Wilton celebrates
THE ROSE
in Cake and Food decorating

My love is like a red red rose
That's newly sprung in June:
My love is like the melodie
That's sweetly play'd in tune
ROBERT BURNS

MARZIPAN ROSES. Cut out petals like cookies, form delicious roses! Party cakes. *Page 4*

STENCIL A ROSE. Give cakes a fresh new look with stenciled roses. Easy! *Page 10*

CANDY ROSES. Sweetest ever—and easy to do. A giant rose, rosy Easter treats. *Page 13*

PIPED ROSES. New short cut roses, classic roses, chocolate roses, rosy treats. *Page 20*

ROSES AND LACE. Perfect partners create perfectly beautiful cakes! *Page 36*

GUM PASTE ROSES…most beautiful of all! A quick new way to make them. *Page 42*

ROMANTIC ROSES. A little treasury of rose-trimmed wedding cakes. *Page 48*

TESTED RECIPES. All you need for confections in this book. Serving guides, too. *Page 60*

ROSE PATTERNS. Find them on the inside covers of this book.

The Romance of the Rose

To the ancient Greeks, the rose was the Queen of Flowers, and so was appropriately the flower of Aphrodite, the Greek goddess of love and beauty. In Roman mythology, Venus was the goddess of love and so, too, the rose was her flower. In Caesar's Imperial Rome, however, the rose became the symbol of *triumphant* love, with victors and revellers alike being adorned with crowns of roses.

Within a short time, the red rose found favor in Christian symbolism, this time as a symbol of martyrdom. The white rose became the symbol of purity. To St. Ambrose is attributed the explanation of how the rose came to have thorns. Before the rose grew on earth, it grew *without* thorns in Paradise. Only after the Fall of Man did thorns appear on the earth-grown rose. The beauty and fragrance of the rose remained as reminders of Paradise lost!

By the Middle Ages, the rose was in full favor in the church. The five petals were identified with Christ's five wounds, the red rose with the blood of the early Christian martyrs. And in Church architecture the rose came into great prominence, particularly in the spectacular "rose" windows of Europe's cathedrals.

In heraldry, the rose has been the perennial favorite. It attained particular prominence during England's savage 30-year War of the Roses, fought under the white rose of the House of York against the red rose of the House of Lancaster. At the war's end the House of Tudor was established through the politic marriage of Lancaster's Henry VII to a York princess. The royal emblem then became the Tudor Rose—a double, with white and red petals representing the two previously feuding houses.

The elaborate Valentines that originated in the Victorian period made the rose a universal symbol of romantic love.

Now you can extend the centuries-old romance of the rose by putting your talents into the creation of a rose-bedecked confection that will carry this message—*here is a tribute of love!*

WILTON BOOK DIVISION STAFF

CO-EDITORS
Marilynn C. Sullivan
Eugene T. Sullivan

CONFECTIONS FASHIONED BY
Wesley Kinsey, senior decorator
Karen Weyhe, decorator

PRODUCTION ASSISTANTS
Ethel LaRoche
James Artman

PHOTOGRAPHY
Tom Kasper

Sixth printing, 7,500, January, 1990

Editorial mail should be addressed to:
    Wilton Book Division
    1603 South Michigan Avenue
    Chicago, Illinois 60616

International Standard Book Number 0-912696-33-8

WILTON ENTERPRISES, INC., WOODRIDGE, ILLINOIS

FRESH ROSES

Loveliest trim you can give to a cake! The delicate perfume and graceful forms of the roses turn dessert into an enchanting centerpiece. When the party's over, present the rose arrangement to the guest of honor.

The fresh rose cake

To set off the rose bouquet, decorating is very simple. The only trim is a series of flounced double ruffles.

1. Bake a cake in a 10½″ ring pan. Ice smoothly in buttercream, then cover with Quick poured fondant (page 60). Divide cake into twelfths and mark at top of side area. Set on serving tray.

2. Pipe a tube 16 shell border at base of cake. At each mark pipe a curved shell with the same tube. From the "tails" of these shells, drop tube 3 strings to define ruffles. Pipe tube 104 ruffled flounces, extending over base border. Top with a second flounce. Start each ruffled flounce just underneath the ruffle previously piped.

3. Arrange the roses. We used a Heart bowl vase which fits the opening in the cake perfectly. Wedge oasis into vase, then moisten with water. Arrange fresh roses and baby's breath by pushing stems into oasis. The flowers will stay fresh for many hours. Cut the cake into twelve servings.

MARZIPAN ROSES

Combine just a few simple ingredients and you've created a delicious substance that's as pliable as modelling clay, that you can roll out just like cookie dough and use to form a beautiful rose!

Wilton marzipan

   8 ounces almond paste
   2 egg whites, unbeaten
   ½ teaspoon vanilla or rum flavoring
   6½ cups sifted confectioners' sugar
      (approximate)

1. Crumble almond paste into a large mixing bowl. Add egg whites and flavoring and knead until thoroughly mixed. Now add the sugar, a cup at a time and knead after each addition until no lumps remain. Add enough sugar to the mixture so that it has the texture of heavy pie dough. The process takes about 20 minutes.

2. Use at once, or wrap in plastic wrap, then put in a tightly closed container and store for months in the refrigerator. When ready to use, bring to room temperature and knead again. If too stiff, knead in a drop or two of warmed corn syrup until original consistency is restored. Yield: 50 to 60 roses.

Basic marzipan techniques

To tint marzipan, break off a portion of the batch and knead in liquid food color, a drop at a time. To tint brown, knead in cocoa. For a rich tan, knead in dry instant coffee powder.

To roll out marzipan, dust work surface and a small rolling pin with a sifting of confectioners' sugar. Roll out just like cookie or pie dough. Cut the rolled marzipan with gum paste cutters or cookie cutters.

To attach a petal, brush egg white on lower edge and press to base.

Always glaze completed marzipan pieces after they have hardened about four hours. The glaze will keep the marzipan fresh and moist.

Corn syrup glaze

Combine ¼ cup light corn syrup and ¼ cup water and heat to boiling in a small saucepan. Brush on marzipan pieces while hot with a pastry or small artist's brush. Dry about 20 minutes.

Modelling the rose

You'll need a fourth-recipe of tinted marzipan, a small rolling pin, confectioners' sugar, plastic wrap, a lightly stirred egg white in a small container and a small artist's brush. To cut the petals, use the medium and large rose petal cutters from the Floral-art set in the gum paste kit.

1. Roll out the marzipan to ⅛" thickness and cut four petals with the medium rose petal cutter and five with the large rose petal cutter. Pick up the scraps, then cover the cut-out petals with plastic wrap. Knead scraps, then form a cone for base— about 1½" x 1" across at the base.

2. Thin one long side of a medium petal by pinching lightly with your fingers. Brush other side with egg white and wrap around the point of the base, starting with the pointed end. Furl the rounded edge of the petal with your fingers. Now add three more medium petals, first thinning as before. These petals should overlap to surround center petal. Furl rounded edge of each as you attach.

3. Now add the five large petals, thinning and furling each. Pinch off the excess marzipan of the base and lay the finished rose on a tray to harden. Cut leaves with a rose leaf cutter, vein with spatula and harden in curved form. Glaze after about four hours. After you've completed one rose, make four or five in assembly-line method.

Marzipan covers a cake side

To give your cake this distinctive and delicious finish, you'll need one recipe of marzipan, wax paper, corn syrup and a plain and a grooved rolling pin. Reserve a small piece of the marzipan for top trim and tint the rest pink.

1. Bake and fill a two-layer 9″ heart cake. Ice in buttercream, smoothing the top carefully.

2. Form a "log" of the pink marzipan, about two feet long. Center on a strip of folded wax paper, 32″ x 6″ wide. Flatten with the plain rolling pin and roll out to about 3″ wide and 32″ long. It should be about ¼″ thick. Dust the grooved rolling pin well with confectioners' sugar and roll again, using a firm, steady pressure.

3. Using a sharp knife and a long straight edge, trim one long side. Following the grooved pattern, trim the short sides to a 32″ length. Using a pastry brush, "paint" the upper side of the cake with corn syrup, leaving the bottom unpainted.

4. Roll up the marzipan, wax paper still attached, making sure the plain, ungrooved side is out. Peel off about a 2″ length of wax paper and gently press the marzipan to the center back of the cake. Holding the rolled marzipan with your left hand, continue unrolling the marzipan as you move around the cake, peeling off the paper with your right hand. The corn syrup will cause the marzipan to adhere to the cake side. Complete covering the cake side, then trim off the strip with a sharp knife. Use a small sharp scissors to cut off the marzipan flush with the top of the cake. Allow the marzipan covering to harden about a half hour, then transfer the cake to a serving tray.

For directions for the top trim of the cake, please turn the page.

Marzipan roses trim party cakes

Make the roses ahead of time (page 4), then pose them on simple cakes for a lavish effect.

Tie up a present

1. Make the rose and four leaves, then set aside to harden. Bake and fill a two-layer 8″ square cake. Make sure the top is level. Ice very smoothly with chocolate buttercream. Set on serving tray. Mark exact center of cake top.

2. Divide a half-recipe of marzipan in two and tint one half yellow, the other green. Roll out yellow marzipan on wax paper. Use a sharp knife to cut into four 2″ wide strips, about 9″ long. Cut right through the wax paper. Cut a point at one end of each strip. Pick up a strip, turn over with wax paper on top and place on cake, point in center. Smooth over cake, pressing lightly against side. Peel off wax paper and trim at base. Do the same with the other strips, forming a cross.

3. Roll out green marzipan on wax paper and cut into 1″ strips, cutting right through paper. Picking up strip and paper as before, press a green strip against base of cake, butting with yellow strip and smoothing around corner. Trim to meet yellow strip on adjacent side. Continue attaching green strips until entire base of cake is bordered. Now add more green strips to form a plaid design, butting with yellow strip on top of cake and working down side. Note that strips do not overlap, but are trimmed where they meet. Attach rose and leaves in center of cake with icing. Serves twelve.

A chocolate ring

Chocolate cake, chocolate icing and delicious pink marzipan roses and buds!

1. Make roses, buds and leaves. Bake a cake in the small ring pan. Ice with chocolate buttercream. The easy way to get a smooth coating is to cover the curved top with tube 402, the sides with giant tube 789. Smooth edges with small spatula. Let icing crust, then cover with chocolate poured fondant.

2. Pipe a bulb border with tube 5. Pipe four tube 3 evenly spaced curves on cake top for stems. Attach roses and buds on dots of icing, then add leaves. Light the candle and serve your delightful Continental cake to twelve.

A celebration sheet cake

1. Make two full marzipan roses and four buds. We chose a fresh peach color to harmonize with the creamy yellow cake. Make eight or ten leaves. Bake a cake in a 7″ x 11″ sheet pan. Ice with buttercream and place on cake board. Cut a 5″ x 7″ oval pattern for plaque and mark on cake top.

2. Tint recipe of marzipan. Roll out to ⅛″ thickness on wax paper. Using pattern, cut out oval plaque, cutting right through wax paper. Pick up plaque, turn over so paper is on top, and lay on cake. Peel off paper.

3. Use the method on page 5 for covering the cake sides with marzipan. After rerolling with grooved rolling pin, cut two strips about 18½″ long and approximately the height of the cake. Cover two adjacent sides of the cake with one strip, then complete covering with second strip.

4. Pipe message with tube 3 and add curved stems with same tube. Now attach roses, buds and leaves with dots of icing. Serves eight, generously.

Quick cut-outs trim a cake *page 5*

If you can cut out cookies, you can create this stylized wild rose design! You will need 2¼″ and 4″ heart cutters and the pansy, forget-me-not and small rose petal cutters from the Floral-art set.

1. From the marzipan you set aside before covering the cake side, tint half green. Divide the remainder in two—tint half yellow, half a delicate blue.

2. Gently press a 2½″ heart cutter in the center of the cake. Press the 4″ heart cutter in the cake to guide the flower trim. Roll out the pink marzipan (left over from covering the side) to ⅛″ thickness. Cut out a 2½″ heart and eleven shapes with the pansy cutter. Cut out twelve blue forget-me-nots and twelve green leaves. Use tubes 7 and 12 to cut out centers for the flowers from yellow marzipan.

3. Place the pink heart in the center of the cake, then arrange the flowers and leaves. Attach centers with a dab of corn syrup. Brush glaze over trim and side of cake. Serve this pretty centerpiece to twelve.

Marzipan roses turn cakes

Wild roses—easy to make

1. Read the directions for rolling marzipan on page 4, then tint about a fourth of a recipe pink and roll out to ⅛″ thickness. Dip the Floral-art pansy cutter in confectioners' sugar and cut out a shape. Place on a square of wax paper.

2. With rounded end of stick 1, gently roll just the center of each petal. This will give them a rounded, cupped form. Place within a curved form (still on wax paper) and harden for several hours. Brush on corn syrup glaze. Use tube 1 and royal icing to pull out stamens in the center. Dry. Your dainty wild rose is finished! You can cut out a dozen or more flowers at once—then shape them in assembly-line fashion. You'll need about 40 for the cake at left. Make about 35 curved marzipan leaves (see page 4).

3. For the candle-holder roses on the top tier, roll the petals as in step 2, then cut a hole in the center of the flower with tube 2A. Surround the hole with stamens.

Make the little tier cake

Any girl will be thrilled with this lofty ruffled creation for her birthday! Use the Mini-tier set and just one cake mix.

1. Bake and ice the three tiers. Place bottom tier on serving tray, two upper tiers on separator plates.

into party centerpieces

2. Use tube 52 to pipe shell borders on top and bottom edges of two lower tiers. Pipe shells on top edge of top tier, then add curved shells with the same tube at the bottom.

3. Divide bottom tier into tenths, mark midway on side, and drop tube 2 strings to define garlands. Pipe the garlands with tube 98 for a triple-ruffled effect. Divide middle tier into tenths, too, and mark just below top border. Drop string guidelines and pipe tube 98 garlands.

4. Now put it all together. Mound icing in center of bottom tier and arrange a cluster of wild roses. Assemble the tiers with clear twist legs. On bottom tier, add more flowers in a cascade, attaching each on a dot of icing. Form a garland of flowers on edge of middle tier. Set candle-holder roses on top tier and push in candles. Trim all the flowers with your made-ahead leaves. Serve this little confection to twelve guests.

A basket of yellow roses

Cover the side of a cake quickly with textured marzipan, heap marzipan roses on top—you've created an old-world masterpiece!

1. Make about two dozen marzipan roses, following directions on page 4. Make a dozen or more curved leaves.

2. Bake and fill a two-layer 8″ cake. Ice all over with yellow buttercream. Make a recipe of marzipan (page 4) and knead in about ½ cup of cocoa.

3. Cover the side of the cake with marzipan just as described on page 5. Use a textured rolling pin for the basket weave effect. You will need a strip about 25″ long. Wrap around cake and trim neatly at top. Set on serving tray. Mound icing on top of cake and press in roses. Add the leaves and the picture is complete! Serve to twelve.

STENCIL A ROSE

Even if you're not a decorator, you can create cakes with a fresh new look by using stencils. The same fashionable clean-cut look that stencils give to furniture, trays, picture frames and other decorative objects can now be applied to cakes.

The process is simple. Trace a stencil from the inside covers of this book on parchment paper. Transfer to light cardboard. The manila folders used for filing are ideal. Cut out the stencil carefully, using an artist's knife with a sharp pointed blade. Now spray the cardboard stencil with non-stick pan release on both sides. Wipe off excess spray. You're ready to begin!

Covering the cake

Either rolled fondant or buttercream is a good background for your stenciled pattern. Start by covering a cake with rolled fondant as the recipe on page 62 directs.

Preparing the "paint"

In a small saucer or ash tray, pour several drops of liquid food color. Add a drop or two of water. Most stencil designs look best in two colors, so prepare another tint in a second saucer. To test the depth of the color, it's best to cover a small cake circle or piece of corrugated cardboard with rolled fondant. This will give you an area to practice on, too. Dab a little of the prepared color on the practice cardboard. If too dark, add a drop of water. Add food color, drop by drop, to deepen the color. We used pink for the roses, green for stem and leaves.

Have at hand a glass of water to clean your brush, a special stencil brush and paper towels.

Applying the design

1. Decide just where to place your stencil by laying the pattern lightly on the cake. If your pattern is repeated (as on the square cake at right) mark corners of the cardboard pattern with a pin.

2. Hold the pattern lightly but firmly on the cake with your fingertips. Dip your brush in the pink color, then touch to a paper towel to remove excess. Holding the brush *straight up*, apply the color to an opening of the stencil. Use a pouncing, up-and-down movement. Do the edges of the open area first, then move to the center. Dip your brush in color and touch to towel as needed.

When you have filled in all the areas of the rose with pink color, lift the cardboard pattern *straight up* off the cake. Gently wipe the stencil on both sides with a damp paper towel to clean it. Pay special attention to the cut edges. Clean your brush

thoroughly in the glass of water and wipe it dry.

3. The pink rose design will be dry in just a few minutes. Now do the green leaves and stems. Lay the cardboard stencil on the cake again. The stenciled pink areas will guide its position. Hold the stencil with your fingertips and apply the green color, just as you did the pink. Lift stencil off, wipe clean and clean your brush.

Tips to remember

1. *Hold your brush straight up* when applying color. Work from edges of opening toward center.

2. *Hold stencil pattern securely* against cake with a light pressure of your fingertips. It is helpful to hold the narrow areas that separate the design (bridges) with the tip of an artist's knife.

3. *Color run under the edge* of the cardboard pattern? Several things could cause this. Perhaps the brush is over-loaded with color. Always tap it on a paper towel before applying to the cake. Also hold the stencil securely against cake with fingertips near the cut edge of the cardboard pattern. Hold the brush vertically, straight up, and use a pouncing motion.

4. *Be sure to clean* both brush and pattern before changing to another color.

5. *For a repeated design* (see the cakes on the next page) do one-fourth of the entire area, then move the stencil to a second, a third and finally a fourth area of the cake top.

6. *Interesting two-tone color* effects can be achieved by repeatedly going over an area with the brush.

Two pretty stenciled cakes

The cakes at right are both covered with rolled fondant that gives a smooth, satiny finish, ideal for applying a stencil design.

The 8" two-layer square cake is graced with a pretty rose pattern repeated four times. A border of curved tube 17 shells completes the trim.

The 10" round cake is trimmed with a graceful rose spray. Instead of white rolled fondant, yellow was used. Food color for stenciling is the same as for the square cake, but the color effect is much different. Add a "braided" border, made from ropes of rolled fondant. Message is piped with tube 2.

Hearts & Flowers stenciled on buttercream cakes

Stenciling on a cake covered with buttercream can be done just the same way as on rolled fondant. The design will have an interesting stippled effect, due to the softness of the icing. The *10" round shower cake* is stenciled this way.

A second way to stencil on buttercream uses a tube, not a brush. Fill a paper cone, fitted with tube 3, with tinted buttercream. Lay cardboard pattern on cake and trace around edges of open areas, then fill in center. Using a small pointed spatula, slide over design in one direction, then slide knife again in opposite direction. Lift off pattern carefully, *straight up*. Allow design to crust about half an hour before applying second tint. *The two 9" x 13" sheet cakes* were done with this method.

CANDY ROSES

Beautifully formed and delicious! Turn the page to see how to make them

Delicate roses made of candy!

Marvelous roses with petals so thin they're translucent! The candy is extremely pliable, so you can furl the petals in any form you wish. Roll it out right on any smooth surface—no confectioners' sugar or grease is needed. To attach a petal, simply press it to its base—it will hold securely. Best of all—the finished flowers are delicious!

Candy for flowers—updated recipe

4½ ounces white Candy Melts™ confectionery
    coating (by weight)
2 drops Candy flavoring
Candy color as desired
2 ounces glucose (by weight)

1. Fill the lower pan of a small double boiler with water to a depth below level of top pan. Bring to a simmer, then remove from heat. Put Candy melts in top pan and stir constantly until melted. Stir in flavoring. Heat glucose just until warm and add to mixture. Stir until thickened and forms a soft ball.

2. Pick up the ball in your hands (it will still be warm) and knead and stretch it like taffy to squeeze out the excess oil. Do this over a pan to catch the oil. After about eight minutes of kneading, wrap the ball tightly in plastic wrap and allow to rest about 45 minutes (or for as long as several days) at room temperature. Kneading out the oil makes the candy stronger and easier to form.

3. When ready to use, knead the mixture briefly, then add color, drop by drop, kneading it in thoroughly. For two or more colors, break off portions of the batch and color separately. Wrap each color in plastic wrap until ready to use. Yield: about 20 roses or 100 wild roses. Recipe may be doubled.

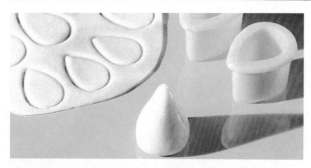

Making a candy rose

You will need the medium and large rose petal cutters, plastic wrap, the small rolling pin and stick 1 from the Gum paste flower kit.

1. Break off a piece of the candy and form into a ball about 1½″ in diameter. Flatten and roll out on smooth surface to 1/16″ thickness. Cut out four petals with the medium cutter, five petals with the large cutter. Pick up the scraps, form into a ball and model into a cone about 1″ high and ¾″ across at base. This is the base of the rose.

BUD

2. Work with one petal at a time, keeping others covered with plastic wrap. Roll the *long side* of one medium petal with the rounded end of the stick to thin it. Roll the stick back and forth over the edge of the petal. Leave other side unthinned. Starting with point of petal, roll around top of base, forming a cone-shape, thinned edge at top. Press lower part of petal to secure to base and furl rounded edge.

Working with three more medium petals, thin *rounded side* of each with the stick. Press pointed sides to base around first petal, overlapping each and furling one side. (Stop here if you want a rosebud and just pinch off excess of base.)

TEA ROSE

FULL BLOWN ROSE

3. Now work with the larger five petals. Thin rounded edge of each by rolling with your stick. Attach below bud. Press a petal to base and furl one side. Press a second petal to base, overlapping first petal and furl. Continue with other three petals. (Picture at top left shows two of the larger petals attached.) Now you have made a tea rose! For a full blown rose, add a row of seven more large petals to base. Complete by pinching off excess candy of base. Set aside to harden overnight.

Making a candy wild rose

1. Easiest of all! Pinch off a small piece of candy and form into a 1″ ball. Flatten and roll out to 1/16″ thickness. Cut out five or six shapes with the pansy cutter from the Gum paste flower kit. Place one on a small square of wax paper, cover others with plastic wrap.

2. Roll each petal with the rounded end of the stick to thin and broaden it. As you finish rolling one petal lift up the edge with the pointed end of the stick, then roll the next petal. Do not roll the center of the flower.

3. Lay flower, still on wax paper, in flower former. Pipe yellow stamens in center with royal icing and tube 1. To make a rose leaf, roll out green candy to 1/6″ thickness. Cut out with a rose leaf cutter, vein by pressing with the edge of a small spatula, and lay in flower former. Harden overnight.

A magnificent Easter egg *shown on page 13*

Mold an egg-shaped box from Candy melts,™ trim it with ribbon and beautiful candy roses, then fill it with homemade chocolates. A sensational Easter surprise! Make the roses in advance.

1. Use the Egg pan set to mold the candy box. For each half-pan you will need four pounds of Candy melts.™ Melt coating as directed in recipe at left and pour into half pan. Support pans on crumpled foil and place on floor of freezer for about 20 minutes. Shell should be hardened but center of egg still soft. Pour out the liquid coating onto foil and return half-eggs to freezer for a few minutes to harden completely. Unmold on paper towels.

2. Place a cookie sheet over a pan of warm water. Set one half-egg on it, rounded side down. In just a few minutes, candy will be melted enough to form a flat base. Harden on wax paper.

3. Trim the open edges of the half-eggs with strips made from contrasting Candy for flowers mixture. Roll out to 1/16″ thickness and cut two ½″ x 12″ strips. Press neatly around edges of half-eggs. Attach ribbon loops for handles. Set top of box upside down. Form a loop at one end of a 9″ length of ribbon. Allow end of loop to extend outside of box, rest of ribbon within box. Fasten by covering with melted coating. Do the same on the other side of the box and harden for several hours.

4. Half-fill a parchment cone with melted coating. Cut tiny opening in tip and write message. Now attach flowers and leaves with melted coating.

For the smaller eggs, below, use the medium mold of the plastic Egg mold set. Mold the same way as the large egg. Attach halves with melted coating.

A giant candy rose

Just spectacular! A true rose with delicate furled petals and a high crown—but big enough to be the centerpiece of a sweet table or the highlight of a big reception. All it takes to make this show piece is the recipe below, a 4″ round cookie cutter and careful advance planning.

Bake the cake

Start by baking a fruit cake in the Wonder mold pan. Set on an 8″ cake circle. The day before you plan to make the rose, ice with buttercream. It is not necessary to smooth icing—just cover the cake.

Prepare the candy

A day in advance, mix this recipe. Mix it four times—do not attempt to double or quadruple the recipe. It would make it too difficult to knead. Measure quantities carefully.

    1 pound white Candy melts™
      confectionery coating
    3 drops Candy color
    6 drops Candy flavoring
    6 ounces glucose, by weight

1. Melt the Candy melts in a double boiler over hot water, stirring constantly (directions on page 14). Stir in color and flavoring.

2. Heat the glucose until just warm and stir it into the melted coating until mixture becomes thick and forms a ball. Now knead to squeeze out the excess oil, just as for the recipe on page 14. Wrap in plastic wrap and set aside.

3. Repeat the recipe three more times. Turn out all four batches on the counter and knead to combine. Wrap tightly in plastic wrap, put in covered container and allow to rest overnight at room temperature.

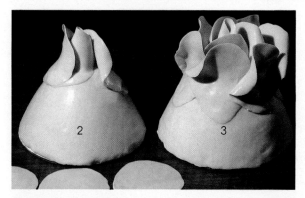

Make the rose

1. Break off about a tenth of the candy and roll out 1/16″ thick, to a rough circle about 14″ in diameter. Drape over cake. Smooth with your hands to cover the cake and trim at base. Reserve scraps to knead back into batch.

2. Cut off half of the remaining candy and roll out to ¼″ thickness. Cut out petals with the 4″ round cutter. Roll out remaining candy to ¼″ thick and cut out more petals. You will need about 32 petals. Knead scraps together and reserve.

Thin one side of each petal by pressing and smoothing with your palm on the counter. Leave other side thick. Attach a petal to the upper part of the cake by pressing and smoothing thick side against cake. Furl thin side of petal to form a cone shape. Attach two more petals, overlapping each and furling thin sides.

3. Attach a second row of six petals just below the three already attached. You'll be surprised at how easy it is to press the petals to the cake and furl the thinned edges. If necessary, go back and furl the petals again, keeping them well up against cake, like a tight bud.

4. Transfer cake to serving tray. Ours is 16″ across. Add a third row of eight petals, attaching just as before. If the petals droop, go back and adjust them—the candy will remain soft and pliable.

5. Attach a final row of 12 or 13 petals near the base of the cake, furling each. These petals will tend to droop, so crumple tissue into balls and prop each petal in the final row. Add more crumpled tissue wherever petals are drooping. Adjust all the petals and harden overnight or longer. Remove tissue.

To serve the cake, remove to kitchen. Pull off petals and place one on each plate. Cut the cake into 30 thin slices and place a slice on each petal.

Candy roses for her birthday

The sweetest birthday cake you could bake is simply decorated—but the candy wild rose trim makes it a little work of art she'll always remember. The delicate pink of the flowers is echoed in the curving baroque borders.

Prepare flowers and cake

1. Make the wild roses and leaves a day or more ahead of time to give them time to harden. Follow the directions on page 15. You'll need about two dozen roses and the same number of leaves.

2. Prepare the tiers. Bake a two-layer 10″ round tier and a single-layer 6″ heart tier. Fill and ice the 10″ layers, ice the heart layer and assemble on serving tray or cake board.

Decorate the cake

1. Divide the 10″ tier into twelfths and mark at base and again 1″ below top edge. Using tube 199 and starting at base, pull up columns all around tier, following marks. With the same tube, pipe large shells, beginning on tier top with tails meeting the tops of the columns. Pipe curved tube 364 shells on either side to form fleurs-de-lis. Drop tube 15 strings from tops of columns. Finish by piping tube 15 rosettes. Fill in between columns on base border with more tube 15 rosettes.

2. On heart tier, pipe tube 14 shell borders at base and top edge. Write your message with tube 2.

3. Now add the candy wild roses in a cascade, attaching each with a dot of icing. Trim the flowers with the delicate leaves. Push in birthday candles, in holders, around the back of the heart tier. Base tier serves 14, upper tier, four guests.

Candy roses for his cake

Curving garlands of rich chocolate buttercream set off the brilliant red candy roses. Serve this showpiece at a party to celebrate a promotion, a retirement, or as a spectacular groom's cake.

Prepare flowers and cake

1. Following directions on page 15, make the candy roses a day or more ahead of time. You will need about six roses and four buds and about 20 leaves.

2. Bake and fill the tiers—a two-layer 9″ x 13″ and a two-layer oval tier. Assemble on cake board.

Decorate the cake

1. On base tier, starting 2½″ in from each corner, divide long sides into fourths and mark midway on sides. On short sides of tier, starting 2½″ in from corners, divide in halves and mark midway on sides. Drop tube 3 strings from mark to mark to define zigzag garlands.

2. On oval tier, make a mark at top center of narrow curved end on each side. Mark 3½″ away from each center mark at top edge. Drop strings from mark to mark to define shallow garlands at ends, deep garlands at center front and back.

3. On base tier, pipe bottom and top shell borders. Pipe zigzag garlands with tube 18 and top with stars piped with same tube.

4. On oval tier, pipe message with tube 2. Pipe a tube 18 bottom shell border. Pipe shallow garlands with tube 18, deep garlands at front and back with tube 21. Finish with a tube 18 top shell border. Arrange roses at either end of tier, attaching with dots of icing. Trim with leaves. Serve base tier to 24 guests, top tier to twelve.

PIPED ROSES...

Even if you've never had a lesson in decorating, you can turn out pretty icing roses like these!

All piped roses, including the classic rose described on page 28, are quick to do—but these are super fast—and lovely enough to pose on a wedding cake.

DROP FLOWER
instant wild rose

SHELL MOTION
quickest rosebud

SPIRAL
quick stylized rose

SHORT CUT RUFFLES
quicker way to
a realistic rose

Drop flower wild roses

Drop tube 33 into a small decorating bag and half-fill with icing of your choice. Cover a cookie sheet with wax paper, securing it with a few dabs of icing. Hold your decorating bag *straight up* in your right hand and touch the tube lightly to the surface. Turn your hand *to the left* as far as possible. Now apply steady pressure as you turn your hand as far as possible *to the right*. Stop pressure, lift bag up. A pretty little wild rose with five perfect petals! For a smaller flower, use tube 225. Add tube 2 dots in center. You can turn out dozens of these roses in just a few minutes. Dry or freeze before placing on cake.

Shell motion rosebud

Drop tube 63 into a small decorating bag and half fill with icing. Cover a cookie sheet with wax paper. Hold the bag at a slant, touch tube lightly to surface. Apply firm pressure to bag, letting icing build up and lifting the tube slightly. Relax your pressure as you pull your hand down. Stop pressure, move away. Dry the rosebuds. Pipe tube 1 stems on cake, then position the buds and add three tube 1 curved lines for stamens.

Stylish spiral rose

Put a little dab of icing on a number 7 flower nail, then put a 2″ square of wax paper on the nail. Use tube 103, the wider end of the tube touching the paper, narrow pointed end straight up. Turn the nail as you apply steady pressure to the bag. Gradually slant the pointed end of the tube outward as you turn. Stop pressure and move tube away. Slide paper, with rose, off nail and place in tray to dry.

Short cut ruffled rose

This is a faster version of the classic rose on page 28. Secure a 2″ square of wax paper to a number 7 flower nail. First pipe a tube 12 cone-shaped mound, holding bag straight up, and lifting tube as the icing builds up. Change to tube 101. Holding tube parallel to the side of the mound, narrow end up, turn nail as you pipe a ribbon of icing around top of cone. Do not stop, but keep turning nail as you pipe a ruffle, moving your hand up and down to make indentations. Keep turning the nail as you pipe ruffles, gradually slanting the narrow end of the tube outward. This non-stop version of the rose rivals the classic rose for beauty. Add more ruffles, or change to a large petal tube for a larger rose.

new quick versions

Icings to use

Royal icing is preferred by most decorators. It holds the crisp forms of the rose petals and produces a strong, easily handled flower. After drying, you can store the roses for weeks, even months. Then they're ready to quickly arrange on the cake on decorating day. By piping a spike of icing on the back of the dried rose, you can push it into the side of a cake and it will hold securely. You can even mount royal icing roses on florists' wire stems to form a bouquet. But large royal icing flowers dry hard, and are usually used as souvenirs for guests—not for eating.

Buttercream roses are good-tasting. By stiffening the icing you can pipe well-formed flowers, then air-dry or freeze them before putting them on the cake top. Chocolate buttercream makes an especially delicious rose.

A combination of half royal icing and half boiled icing is good for piping roses, too. The boiled icing is light, so less pressure is needed. The finished roses may be made ahead, dried and stored, but they are not as strong as those piped in royal icing.

Quick rosebuds circle a cake

Here's another quick way to pipe a rosebud in a few seconds. Here they accent the bold curves that swing around the cake and serve as candle holders. We recommend buttercream to cover the cake and for the rosebuds, boiled icing for the borders.

1. Pipe about 30 rosebuds in advance. These are really rosettes. Fit a small decorating bag with tube 20 and half fill with buttercream. Cover a cookie sheet with wax paper. Hold your bag straight up and touch the tube lightly to the surface. Apply even pressure as you move your hand in a tight circular movement from center around to outer edge. Tuck tube under to finish. These are almost as fast as drop flowers. Freeze or air-dry while you prepare the cake.

2. Bake and fill a two-layer 8″ round cake. Ice smoothly in buttercream and place on serving tray. Divide cake side into tenths and mark 1″ above base. Mark again on top edge. (A cake dividing set makes this easy.)

3. Starting at marks, pipe long curved shells around base of cake with tube 32 and boiled icing. Go back and cover with a second layer of shells, starting just above first series. Pipe a star between each shell at base. Use tube 152 to pipe the top border, just as you did the base border. Add stars.

4. Attach rosebuds at each curved shell, securing with dots of icing. Trim the rosebuds with tube 66 leaves. Arrange a circle of rosebuds in center of cake and push in birthday candles. Serve this rosy treat to twelve.

Quick rosebuds trim festive treats

Dainty pastel icing and sweet rosebud trim turn a tray of little pastries into a delightful party centerpiece. Here's how to create it.

Rosebud cookie cornucopias

Pipe buttercream "rosette" rosebuds ahead of time with tube 16 (page 21). Air-dry or freeze. Bake and form the cookies, using the recipe for Cookie cornucopias on page 61. Cool thoroughly. To fill the cookies, fit a 12″ decorating bag with tube 508 and fill with Stabilized whipped cream (page 62). Pipe the cream into the cornucopias, holding cookie in your left hand, decorating bag in your right hand. End with a swirl. Trim by gently pressing in a rosebud, then adding a tube 65 buttercream leaf. *Note:* Fill and decorate the cookies no earlier than three hours before serving. Refrigerate until time to serve.

Rosebud cupcakes

Pipe classic rosebuds (page 28) with tube 102 and buttercream. Freeze or air-dry. Use your favorite recipe to bake small cupcakes. Cool, then swirl tops with Buttercream or Boiled icing—egg white (page 60). Pipe a curved tube 2 stem on each cake. Set rosebud on a dot of icing and pull out tube 2 lines for calyx. Add tube 65 leaves.

Rosebud petits fours

Appealing little cakes that you can vary endlessly with flavors of cake, filling and icing. In advance pipe tube 63 shell-motion buttercream rosebuds (page 20). Air-dry or freeze. Bake your favorite cake recipe in a 12″ x 18″ pan with 1″ raised edges. Turn out cake and cut in half to form two 9″ x 12″ layers. Chill layers, then fill with recipe of your choice. We used raspberry jam. Trim off crusty edges and cut into 1½″ wide strips, then diagonally into diamonds. Ice cakes with white buttercream and let icing crust about half an hour. Cover with Quick poured fondant, page 60. Let fondant set. Attach rosebuds on dots of icing, pipe tube 2 calyxes and stems, then tube 65 leaves. Place in fluted paper cups to serve. Yield: 35 petits fours.

Yellow rosebud party cake

Quick pretty rosebuds trim this cake that features an unusual shape. The simplest of borders completes the trim.

1. Pipe the shell-motion rosebuds in advance in royal icing as directed on page 20. Dry. You will need five or six larger tube 62 rosebuds for cake top, about 24 smaller tube 63 rosebuds for side of cake. Set aside to dry.

2. Bake a layer in a 10″ round pan and one in a 10″ top bevel pan. Fill the layers, then ice smoothly in buttercream—top yellow, sides white. Divide cake into twelfths and mark 1½″ above base and at top of bevel slant. Place on serving tray.

3. Write name on cake top with tube 1. Pipe a spray of stems with tube 2, then curved stems on bevel slant with same tube, starting at marks. Pipe all shell borders with tube 16. Pipe tube 104 swags around base of cake from mark to mark.

4. Attach rosebuds on dots of icing. Do calyxes with tube 2, perky leaves with tube 66. (Thin icing with corn syrup for leaves.) Serve to 14 party guests.

Quick rosy trims for love cakes

A pretty cake is such a sweet way to show your love—and roses are the flower of love. Study this quartet of rose-trimmed cakes, then decorate your own love cake for Valentine's day, an engagement announcement, or just to show you care.

Ruffled roses, ruffled tiers

Three little heart-shaped tiers are decked with a quick new version of the double wild rose.

1. Make new ruffled royal icing wild roses in advance. Attach a 2″ square of wax paper to a number 7 flower nail with icing. Use tube 102, holding narrow pointed end out, tube almost parallel with nail, to pipe a continuous ruffled circle as you turn nail. Move your hand in and out to simulate five petals. There will be an empty space in the center of the circle. Pipe a smaller circular ruffle on top of the first, holding the narrow end of the tube slanted slightly upward. Slide paper off nail and lay within flower former to dry. After you've piped about 30 double wild roses, add stamens to all with tube 1s. Dry.

2. Bake the three tiers in Heart mini-tier pans. Place each on a corrugated cardboard base cut to fit, then ice with buttercream. Place base tier on serving tray and set middle tier on it. Set top tier on separator plate, assemble with legs and push legs into middle tier down to cardboard base beneath it. Divide each side of base tier into sixths and mark midway on side. Drop tube 2 strings from mark to mark to guide ruffles.

3. Decorating is fast and fun. Pipe tube 15 shell borders at bottom and top of all tiers. On base tier pipe ruffled garlands with tube 104. On middle tier, pipe tube 104 ruffles over the shell border at top of tier. Use tube 104 again to pipe a ruffle at bottom of top tier, lifting ruffle at point of heart. Mound a little icing on tops of middle and top tiers, then arrange roses on cake as picture shows. Add a few tube 66 leaves and serve to twelve.

Hearts and rosebuds on a cake top

Symbols of romance trim a very feminine cake.

1. Pipe the quick shell-motion rosebuds in advance in royal icing using tube 62. Use the directions on page 20.

2. Bake, fill and ice a two-layer 10″ cake. Use a 2″ heart cookie cutter to lightly press eight evenly spaced heart designs around cake top. Using these designs as guides, mark cake side 1″ below top edge. Drop tube 2 string guidelines for garlands from mark to mark.

3. On cake top, use tube 16 to outline heart designs. Pipe tube 16 bottom and top shell borders, then pipe the ruffled garlands with tube 88. This tube pipes a ruffle and a zigzag heading all at once.

4. Pipe three tube 2 stems within each heart, and short stems above points on garlands. Attach rosebuds on dots of icing, then add clusters of tube 66 leaves. Serve your love cake to 16.

Be my love

A big, beautiful Valentine, very quickly created. Fast ruffled roses are the trim.

1. Pipe eight quick ruffled roses and four buds in buttercream. Follow the directions on page 20. Air-dry or freeze.

2. Bake a cake in the Double-tier heart pan. Ice in buttercream, then cover with Quick poured fondant. Let icing crust, then pipe tube 2 message, tube 17 bottom shell border. Attach flowers with dots of icing and trim with tube 68 leaves. Serve to twelve.

Stylish little Valentines

Glossy little heart cakes, dainty roses!

1. Make the quick spiral roses with tube 102 in buttercream. Follow the directions shown on page 20. Air-dry or freeze.

2. Bake the little cakes in Heart mini-cake pans. Ice in buttercream and cover with poured fondant. Arrange trios of roses on top and trim the roses with tube 65 leaves.

More quick ways to pipe

A birthday doll

Any little girl will fall in love with this pretty doll! She holds a rose in her hands and is dressed in ruffles to look like a great big rose!

1. For the base the doll stands on, bake a single-layer 10″ round cake. Ice and place on serving tray. Divide into eighths and mark on top edge. Gently press a 6″ cake circle on top to mark a circle. Insert six ¼″ dowel rods, evenly spaced, around circle. Lift out, clip off level with top of cake, and push in again. This will support weight of doll cake.

2. For the doll's skirt, bake a cake in a Wonder mold pan. Place on 8″ cake circle. Ice a marshmallow to top to lengthen the waist. Insert Little girl doll pick. Paint bodice area of doll pick with thinned icing, then ice the wonder mold cake, filling in around marshmallow for a smooth line. Divide and mark bottom into sixths. With a toothpick, draw lines from marks to waistline. Place doll on base cake. Now you're ready to decorate!

3. Pipe a tube 16 shell border around bottom of doll cake. The skirt is ruffled with five sizes of petal tubes, so use a decorating bag with a coupler so you can change tubes. Starting at hem, pipe tube 127 ruffles in a curve from mark to mark around skirt. Top with two more rows of tube 127 ruffles. Continue with three rows of tube 125 ruffles, four rows of tube 124, five rows of tube 104 and four rows of tube 103. Wire doll's hands together, then pipe a tube 102 ruffled collar.

4. On base cake, pipe a shell border, then add tube 104 ruffled garlands from mark to mark. Insert candles in Push-in holders and pipe tube 67 leaves. For a final touch, pipe a tiny tube 101s rose on a florists' wire, tie with ribbons and insert in doll's hands. Base cake serves eight, doll cake serves twelve guests.

A rose covers a cake!

Easy to do, because the petal shape of the cake guides the piping. Very pretty to view with the ruffly petals shading from pale to deep pink.

1. Bake and fill a 12″ two-layer petal cake. Ice in pale pink buttercream. Run a tube 16 line around the base of the cake and use the same tube to pipe a top shell border.

2. Using the same icing and tube 127, pipe three rows of petals on cake top, starting at outer edge and working in. Tint remaining icing a deeper pink and add three more rows of petals with tube 126. Add more color to remaining icing and pipe a final three rows of ruffles with tube 124. Pipe a spiral

pretty rose cakes

disk of yellow icing in center, then pull out stamens with tube 2. Finish with a tube 112 shell motion bottom border and tube 112 leaves. Serve to 26.

Rosebud kids...

Fun for a shower and very quick to decorate!

1. Bake and ice a 12" x 18" sheet cake. Bake two single-layer oval cakes. Ice sides white, tops peach color. Place sheet cake on cake board and pipe tube 16 shell borders. Place oval cakes on cardboard bases cut to fit.

2. Pipe tube 16 base borders around oval cakes, then add a double tube 127 ruffle around each cake top. Edge ruffles with tube 3 bulbs. For features, pipe tube 5 eyes and noses, tube 4 smiles and tube 12 round cheeks. Do boy's hair and girl's curls with tube 17. Place oval cakes on sheet cake.

3. Finish with tube 127 bows and tube 18 rosette rosebuds—blue for the boy, pink for the girl. Add bows to the sheet cake, too. Serve the sheet cake to 26, oval cakes to twelve guests.

How to pipe a classic rose

The time-honored Wilton way of piping a rose hasn't changed. It's a two-step method that produces a realistic rose in an efficient way—a rose you can vary endlessly by adding petals, using a larger or smaller petal tube, or modifying to produce an icing replica of a named variety. Many thousands of Wilton school students have learned this technique in just a few minutes. Here's how they do it.

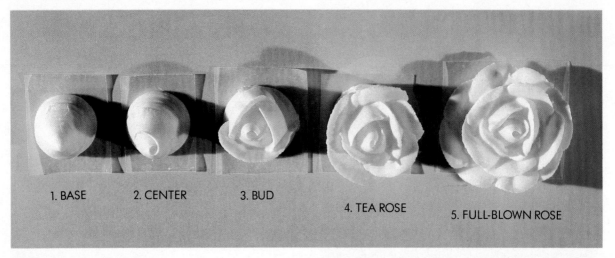

1. BASE   2. CENTER   3. BUD   4. TEA ROSE   5. FULL-BLOWN ROSE

Piping a classic rose

1. Attach a 2″ square of wax paper to a number 7 flower nail with a dot of icing. Using tube 12 and either royal or stiffened buttercream (page 60) pipe a tube 12 cone-shaped mound of icing. Hold the tube straight up, vertically, and apply steady pressure as the icing builds up. Keep the tip of the tube buried in the icing. When the cone is about ¾″ high, stop pressure and lift tube away. You have formed the base of the rose.

2. Now change to tube 104. Hold the tube parallel to the tip of the base, wider end down, and pipe a spiral ribbon of icing around the base, turning the nail as you pipe. This is the center of the rose.

3. Add three petals. Touch tube to base below spiral. As you turn the nail, lift the tube up, then down to form a petal. Starting in the center of the first petal, repeat the motion, then repeat it again, starting in center of second petal. Repeat again. You have formed a rose bud.

4. For a tea rose, add five petals, each overlapping. Press the wide end of the tube against the base, starting farther down. Now hold the tube with narrow end flaring outward from the base. Pipe five overlapping petals with quick up-down movements of your hand.

5. For a full-blown rose, pipe seven more overlapping petals. This time, hold the tube almost horizontal. When you have finished, slide the wax paper square off the nail and onto a tray to dry. The first rose you pipe is always a beautiful surprise—it looks so real!

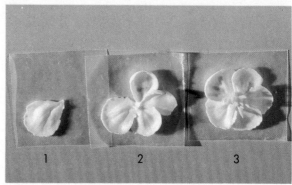

1   2   3

Piping a wild rose

1. Attach a small square of wax paper to a number 7 nail with a dot of icing. Use tube 104 and either royal or stiffened buttercream icing. Touch the wide end of the tube to the center of the nail, holding the tube almost parallel to the nail's surface. Apply even pressure as you move your hand out and then in again. You will form a rounded, slightly cupped petal.

2. Pipe four more petals, turning the nail as you pipe. Make sure they overlap each other.

3. Pull out a cluster of tube 1 yellow stamens in the center. Slide the paper off the nail. Dry either on a flat surface or within a flower former to give a lift to the petals. The wild rose is the quickest and easiest flower to pipe on a nail—and one of the prettiest.

Golden roses on an oval cake

A simple cake becomes a showpiece when it's trimmed with two-tone classic roses.

1. Pipe the two-tone roses. For this effect have two decorating bags of icing ready—one filled with deep yellow icing for the center bud of the rose and another filled with paler yellow icing for the outer petals. For this cake you will need two tube 124 big roses, three tube 104 roses and eight deep yellow rosebuds. Dry.

2. Bake a two-layer oval cake. Fill and ice with buttercream. Divide cake into twelfths and mark midway on side. Pipe a tube 16 bottom shell border. Drop tube 14 strings from mark to mark, omitting two strings at center front of oval. Top strings with rosettes. For top border, pipe a line all around the edge of the cake with tube 14. Cover the line with shells. Now pipe two more rows of shells, one on either side of first row.

3. Arrange the roses in curves as picture shows, attaching with mounds of icing. Pipe tube 2 curved stems, then attach rosebuds. Finish with tube 66 leaves. This little showpiece serves twelve.

Ruffles and wild roses

This beguiling little cake frames dainty wild roses with rows of double ruffles.

1. Pipe a dozen wild roses with tube 104 and royal icing. Center with tube 1 stamens. Dry within a flower former.

2. Bake, fill and ice a two-layer 8″ square cake. Starting 2″ in from each corner, make a mark on each side of cake ½″ below top edge. Make a mark in exact center of each side of cake ½″ above bottom. Connect marks for triangle design to guide ruffles. Mark a 5″ circle on cake top.

3. Pipe tube 16 shell borders at bottom and top of cake. Use pale and deep yellow icing for the ruffles. With tube 104, pipe a deep yellow ruffle, following marks on side of cake. Top with a pale yellow ruffle. Following marked circle on cake top, pipe a deep yellow ruffle. Within it, pipe a pale yellow ruffle. Now attach the flowers on mounds of icing. Add precisely placed leaves with tube 68. This tailored treat serves twelve.

Classic roses, classic cakes

Rose cascade *top right*

A beautiful cake with a sweet old fashioned air. Precisely piped borders set off the delicate rose cascades.

1. Pipe tube 104 roses in royal icing as shown on page 28. Pipe tiny wild roses with tube 101. Set aside to dry. Pipe a tube 10 "spike" on the backs of six roses. Dry.

2. Bake a 10″ round, two-layer cake, each layer 2″ high. Fill and ice with buttercream and set on serving tray. Divide side into twelfths and mark 1½″ above base. Drop string guidelines for garlands. Press a 4″ cookie cutter in center of cake top.

3. Pipe a tube 17 shell bottom border. Do ruffled garland with tube 104, holding narrow end of tube almost straight out for a flouncy effect. Pipe zigzag garland above it with tube 17. Drape the garlands with tube 2 strings, adding loops and spiral knots at points.

4. Using marked circle as guide, pipe tube 16 scallops on cake top. Add rosettes at points. Do top shell border with same tube. Now arrange the roses in six cascades. Pipe a mound of icing on spikes and push roses into cake side. Add more roses on cake top on dots of icing and fill in with wild roses and tube 66 leaves. Push in a slender taper for a birthday or just for sparkle. Serve to 14.

Birthday roses *lower right*

Dress up an easy petal cake with fluffy garlands and classic roses that double as candle holders.

1. Pipe the royal icing roses with tube 104 petals just as shown on page 20. After you have piped the tube 12 mound, push a birthday candle into it. Then proceed to add the petals. Slide paper off nail to dry and adjust candle so it is vertical.

2. Bake, fill and ice a two-layer 12″ petal cake. Pipe message on cake top with tube 1. Place on serving tray and pipe a tube 16 base shell border. Pipe tube 21 zigzag garlands and top with curved shells. Do top border the same way, using tube 18. Set rose candles on mounds of icing. Light the candles and serve to 16 guests.

Wild rose garland *below*

Once you have gained the technique of piping classic roses, you can modify the petals and add details to produce an almost exact replica of a named variety. This lovely cake is graced with "Lord Penzance" roses, unusual and much-loved flowers.

1. Make the roses in royal icing with tube 125. Add a little width to the petals, giving them a slight ruffle and keeping them well overlapped. Indent center of each petal with an artist's brush. Pipe a tube 5 yellow ball in the center and flatten with your fingertip. Lay flower within flower former. Pipe clusters of many upright yellow stamens with tube 1s. Dry. Pipe a few rosebuds with tube 104. After drying add tube 2 pointed calyxes.

2. Bake a 10″ x 3″ cake, using a firm pound cake or fruit cake recipe. Cover with Rolled fondant. (Directions on page 62.) Now arrange your "Lord Penzance" roses in a garland, attaching with dots of icing. Pipe tube 67 leaves. Serve your little work of art to 14.

31

Charming Victorian roses

Ruffles and garlands, ribbons and lace give quaint charm to these dainty cakes. Each is set off by precisely piped classic roses.

Start each cake by covering a two-layer 8″ square with glossy poured fondant (page 60). Each serves twelve party guests.

Victorian lace *at left*

1. Mark a 4″ circle with a cookie cutter in center of cake top. Mark a 2″ strip extending from circle down each side of cake. Using pattern on inside cover and straight pin, mark both edges of strip where lattice forms a point. Start tube 1s lattice by dropping a line from the first mark at one edge of a strip to the fifth mark at the opposite edge. Continue dropping parallel diagonal lines until you reach the base of the cake, then go back and pipe lines in the opposite direction.

2. Add tube 41 double scallops, using lattice as guide. Pipe tube 2 tear drops, tube 1 dots. Do stylized flowers on lattice with tube 2 tear drops. Pipe a tube 4 bulb border at base. Finish by arranging a cluster of five tube 102 roses in center of cake. Trim with tube 66 leaves.

Cameo rose *top right*

1. Pipe twelve perfect tube 102 roses and about 144 tube 124 drop flowers. Mark a 5″ circle on cake top. Starting 2″ in from each corner, make a mark ¾″ below cake top. Make a second series of marks 1″ below first marks. Drop guidelines from lower marks for ruffles.

2. Pipe a tube 4 bottom bulb border. Do ruffles with tube 104, edge with tube 2 beading. Drop tube 2 strings from upper marks, then add tiny tube 1 scallops. Arrange flowers in precise curves and scatter tube 1 dots around them. Finish by trimming with tube 65 leaves.

Ruffles and roses *bottom right*

1. Pipe two-tone roses, each with a spike—four with tube 104, 12 with tube 103 and eight with tube 102. Pipe eight tube 102 rose buds. Divide each side of cake into thirds and mark at top edge. Drop strings from marks to guide ruffles.

2. Pipe a tube 16 bottom shell border and tube 104 ruffles. Attach roses, largest at corners, and add tube 65 leaves. Tie up your pretty cake with tube 102 blue bows.

Chocolate roses!

Is there a man (or woman or child) who doesn't love chocolate? To make your chocolate lover supremely happy, bake him one of these handsome chocolate cakes. Use your favorite chocolate cake recipe, cover the cake with rich chocolate icing, add bold borders. For the final touch, luscious chocolate roses!

To the groom!

A chocoholic's dream! This cake is planned for the wedding reception table to set off the snowy tiers of the bridal cake, but it's a superb confection for any party occasion.

1. Pipe the classic chocolate roses in Chocolate buttercream. You'll need six tube 104 roses for the sides of the cake and four big tube 124 roses for the corners. You may need to stiffen the icing with additional confectioners' sugar to help the petals hold their shapes. Freeze or air-dry.

2. Prepare the cake. Bake a chocolate cake recipe in the Long loaf pan. We suggest you chill the cake, then slice it into two layers with a long serrated knife. For filling, use the recipe for Chocolate Continental butter cream. Ice the cake with Buttercream, chocolate flavored. Let the icing crust, then give the cake a coating of Chocolate poured fondant. (Double the recipe for this cake.) Let icing harden, then set on cake board.

3. Use Chocolate buttercream for decorating. Pipe message with tube 3. Divide the long sides of the cake into fourths and mark midway on sides. Drop string guidelines for garlands from mark to mark. Pipe the big fluted garlands with giant tube 2E. Pipe a ruffled tube 112 leaf at each point, then a tube 18 rosette. Attach the roses with dots of icing and trim with more leaves. This wonderful cake serves 16 chocolate lovers.

A chocolate hexagon for Dad

An easy-to-decorate cake because the shape guides the piping—very little measuring is needed.

1. Pipe about 25 roses and a few buds with tube 104 and Chocolate buttercream. Air-dry or freeze. Use buttercream for the plaque, too. Stiffen about a cup of the icing with additional confectioners' sugar. Form into a ball, flatten and roll out to 1/8" thickness between sheets of wax paper. Remove top layer of paper and cut out with a 4" round cookie cutter. Refrigerate, still on paper, until time to place it on the cake.

2. Bake a two-layer cake in 12" hexagon pans. Fill with smooth, rich Continental chocolate butter cream. Set on cake board. Ice the cake and do trims with Chocolate buttercream.

3. Place plaque on cake top. (Turn over so wax paper is on top, place on cake and peel off paper.) Write message with tube 2. Divide each side of cake into thirds and mark at top edge. Drop tube 16 strings from mark to mark. At each corner of cake, pipe a tube 22 shell, starting on cake top, then pulling down the side into a column. Pipe tube 18 bottom and top shell borders. Edge plaque with tube 4 bulbs. Now add the handsome roses, attaching with dots of icing. Trim with tube 68 leaves. Serve your delicious creation to 18 guests, cutting each side into three slices.

The airy, see-through look of lace is a perfect partner for roses—one sets off the other for a perfectly beautiful cake! The loveliest example of a lace-trimmed cake is one done in the Australian style.

Double-ring Australian Rose

Here lace is used in three ways—in the delicate freehand lace "embroidery," the dainty lace pieces and in the cloud-like "curtaining" that circles the lower tier. The only non-traditional touch is the graceful ring shape of the tiers. An arrangement of beautiful gum paste roses crowns the cake.

Make Australian Rose for a small wedding reception, or for the centerpiece of an important party. You will need 10″ and 14″ plates from the Tall tier set, a 6½″ center column, a top cap nut and three legs. Glue the legs to the bottom of the 14″ plate. You will also need a petite ornament base. Turn the base upside down and glue it to the plate to form a bowl.

Work in advance

1. Make the gum paste roses. Page 44 shows you how. You will need six full-blown roses, five tea roses, eight buds and 20 leaves. Cover a styrofoam ball with royal icing and secure it in your prepared vase with more icing. Now arrange your flowers and leaves by pushing wire stems into the ball.

2. Pipe the lace pieces. Use the patterns on inside cover and directions on the next page. Use Egg white—royal icing and tiny tube 0L. You will need about 100 larger pieces and about 60 small pieces, but make extras in case breakage occurs.

3. Bake the cake—smaller tier in the 8″ ring pan, larger tier in the 10½″ ring pan. Australian cakes are made of fruit cake batter, but you may substitute a firm pound cake recipe.

Cover the cake

1. In the Australian tradition cakes are given a double covering—first with marzipan, then with rolled fondant. For this cake, you will need two recipes of marzipan, page 4. Set each tier on a cake circle cut to size and shape. Attach with a few strokes of icing. Fill in any cracks or holes by pressing in small pieces of marzipan. Prepare an apricot glaze by heating two cups of apricot preserves to boiling. Strain, then brush over tiers while still hot. Meanwhile, roll out about two-thirds of the marzipan to a circle about 20″ in diameter, ¼″ thick. Drape over lower tier, letting marzipan fall loosely into center hole. Smooth with your hands over tier. Cut an "X" in marzipan over hole, and ease over sides of hole. Patch if necessary. Trim off neatly at base. Cover top tier the same way. Allow to dry 48 hours so oil in marzipan will not discolor fondant covering.

2. Brush marzipan-covered tiers with glaze. Now make a double recipe of rolled fondant, page 62.

Roll out about two-thirds of it to a 20″ circle, ¼″ thick, and smooth over lower tier, just as you did with the marzipan. Trim off excess at base, smooth again with your palms and trim again. Cover top tier the same way. This double covering will keep your tiers fresh and moist for weeks. The smooth surface gives a perfect base for decorating.

Decorate lower tier

1. Assemble 14″ plate with column and place tier on it. Divide side into 16ths and mark 1″ above base. Trace curtaining pattern on parchment paper and transfer to side of tier, matching one lower corner of triangular pattern to each mark. Prick pattern with a pin to transfer.

2. Pipe freehand stylized roses between each marked pattern with tube 0L and royal icing. These designs are only about ½″ across. Following pattern on side, pipe freehand flower design on tier top. Pipe a tube 5 bottom bulb border.

3. Pipe extensions or "shelves" for curtaining. Use tube 2 and royal icing. First pipe a curved line the full width of each triangle. Go back and pipe a shorter line, centering it on first line. Continue until you have piped a total of four lines, each shorter than the one before. After you have piped two lines, let icing dry before piping the next. Pipe a finishing line around each curve. Dry, then brush surface of extensions with thinned icing. Dry.

4. Do curtaining with tube 0L and Egg white—royal icing. Thin icing with corn syrup until it flows easily from the tube. Drop a string from point of pattern to center of extension. Fill in with strings on either side, keeping strings vertical and closely spaced. Dry, then edge with "snail's trails" (tiny bulbs) and scallops. Drop scallops from edges of extensions.

5. Attach lace pieces, inner circle first. Pipe tube 0L dots of icing on back of a larger lace piece and gently hold to cake for a second until icing sets. Be sure to keep all pieces at a uniform angle. Next, attach pieces to outer circle.

Decorate top tier

1. Set tier on 10″ plate, then on turntable. Support with crumpled foil. Divide into 16ths and mark midway on side. Following marks, pipe freehand flower motifs with tube 0L and royal icing. Corresponding to side designs, pipe flower motifs on top of tier. Pipe a tube 4 bottom bulb border. Secure tier to center column with nut. Attach smaller lace pieces, starting at inner ring, just as you did for lower tier.

2. Set the rose arrangement on top tier. Australian Rose is exquisite! At a wedding reception, slice upper tier into 20 servings, lower tier into 30 servings. Or serve to 25 guests at a party.

Lace…lovely, easy to do

While even the simplest touch of lace on a cake appears difficult to do, piping lace is really an easy technique. If you can drop an icing string, you can pipe even the most elaborate lace cake trim.

Lace done right on the cake is very quick and easy. The "lace embroidery" on the Australian cake, page 36 is a good example. Even faster to do is the delicate veil of Philippine-style "sotas" shown on the opposite page and on page 43.

Lace piped off the cake can take various forms. It can be flamboyant lace wings derived from South African decorating, where the lace rises above the cake for an air-borne effect. It can be as dainty as tiny lace pieces, applied one by one to a cake for the most fragile effect. See again the Australian cake on page 36.

Lace can be three-dimensional, standing out from the cake in cobwebby curves. Lace pieces can be curved, then assembled into flower-like forms. Explore all the various ways of the magic of lace —then adorn show piece cakes with lace. They'll excite lots of admiration—and win prizes, too. You won't need to admit how easy it was to give the lovely look of lace to your masterpieces.

Most important—the correct icing

All lace is piped with tiny tubes, ranging from tube 000 for thread-like forms to tube 2 for a slightly bolder effect. Therefore, it's important to use an icing that's thin enough to pass easily through the small openings of these tubes, yet strong enough to hold the graceful curves. If the icing is too stiff it will be difficult to press through the tube and result in clumsy looking curves. If the icing is too thin, it will collapse, and not have the strength to hold its form.

For lace piped right on the cake, use a very flexible, easy-to-pipe icing. Boiled icing is best for sotas. It just seems to fly out of the tube to produce fine glossy curves and curls that quickly cover the surface. Use either Boiled icing—meringue or Boiled icing—egg white, pages 60-61. Thin with a little light corn syrup or piping gel. Practice piping off the cake—then add the syrup or gel drop by drop if the icing seems a bit too stiff. For free-hand embroidery, you will need to pipe a bit more slowly. Use royal icing, thinned as necessary with piping gel or corn syrup. Experiment to bring the icing to the consistency that's easiest for you to pipe, yet will hold clear-cut curves.

For lace piped off the cake you will need a very strong icing. Royal icing will be your choice. It holds clear-cut curves that follow a pattern accurately, and drys to a durable form that you can pick up and place on the cake. Either Royal icing—meringue or Royal icing—egg white is suit-able (page 60). Royal—egg white is a little stronger and is the best choice for very fine patterns.

How to pipe lace wings

This is just tracing in icing. Trace the pattern (on inside cover of this book) accurately on parchment paper. Repeat the tracing several times, for you will need a number of wings. Tape edges of your traced pattern smoothly to a stiff surface. A piece of glass or plexiglass is perfect. Over the patterns, tape wax paper, making sure it is smooth. Now pipe the design on the wax paper. Hold your tube slightly above the surface so the thread of icing drops into the pattern curves. Dry thoroughly, at least several hours, depending on the humidity of your work area. To remove the lace wings, cut around edges of the wax paper with an artist's knife. Run a thin card under the wax paper. Designs will loosen and may be picked up to place on the cake. They *are* fragile—so always pipe extras in case of breakage.

How to pipe small lace pieces

Do this just like piping a lace wing. Estimate how many lace pieces you will need for your cake—then trace the pattern as many times as necessary, keeping the tracings in rows. Cover with wax paper, pipe designs, dry and loosen, just as for wings.

How to pipe curved lace

This is just as easy as piping wings. Tape your traced patterns to either the inner or outer surface of a flower former. Tape wax paper smoothly over the patterns, pipe the designs. Dry thoroughly, then cut the edges of the wax paper with a sharp knife and slide the wax paper, still holding piped designs, onto a towel-covered surface. Curved designs may be easily picked up, then assembled, as shown in the wild rose cake on page 40. Pipe extras in case of breakage.

Three-dimensional lace trims

See the cake on the top of page 41. The curved, two-sided forms seem almost impossible for icing to perform—but it's really easy with Australian nails. Grease the nail lightly but thoroughly with solid white vegetable shortening. Hold the stem of the nail with your left hand as you pipe free-hand lattice and designs with your right hand.

Be sure to keep the piping ⅛″ above the open edge of the nail. Stick the stem of the nail into a block of styrofoam to dry. Now place the styrofoam, with nails, into a warm oven for just a minute or two. Leave the oven door open. The gentle heat will melt the shortening and you can easily push the piped design off the nail into your palm.

Sotas lace veils a party cake *below*

1. Pipe the Classic roses with tube 104 and royal icing. Dry, then pipe a tube 9 spike on the backs of six of the roses. Dry again. These will go on the sides of the cake.

2. Bake and fill a 12″ x 4″ hexagon cake. Ice with buttercream. Make an oval pattern, 4″ x 2¾,″ and transfer to cake sides. Fold a 9″ circle of parchment paper into sixths, fan fashion. Cut a curve on open end to make a scalloped pattern. Transfer to cake top. Outline patterns with tube 3 strings.

3. Using boiled icing and tube 1s, cover the cake with sotas up to the patterns. Hold the tube a little above the surface and pipe curves, "C" shapes and loops, using light steady pressure. Go back and cover the corners again.

4. Finish the cake by piping tube 2 beading around patterns, a tube 5 ball border and fleurs-de-lis at base. Pipe a mound of icing on top and arrange roses. Push spiked roses on mounds of icing into sides. Add tube 67 leaves. Serve to 20 guests.

A trio of lacy rose cakes

Aren't they lovely? See how the ethereal touch of lace adds beauty to a simply-decorated cake. Pipe the lace in advance, then the cakes are quick to do.

A rosy winged tier cake

1. Pipe the two-tone roses and buds in royal icing with tubes 104 and 102. Dry. Pipe the lace wings in royal icing with tube 2, following pattern. You will need eight, but make a few extra in case of breakage. Dry thoroughly.

2. Bake and fill a two-layer 12″ petal tier and a single-layer 6″ petal tier. Ice in buttercream and assemble on serving tray. Pipe tube 14 shell borders at base of both tiers. Do elongated curved shells at base of 12″ tier with tube 21. Pipe similar curved shells at top edge of tier with same tube. Do not allow the shells to touch at indentations of tier—allow ¼″ space for lace wings. Decorate top tier same as bottom tier, using tube 16.

3. Mound icing on cake top and press in roses. Attach rosebuds to base of cake. Trim with tube 69 leaves. Now for the lace! Pipe dots of icing where

lace wings will rest on cake. Gently press wings to cake. Serve your winged showpiece to 32 guests.

"Petticoat" lace on a yellow rose cake

1. Pipe the three-dimensional lace pieces on Australian crescent nails just as directed on page 38. Use tube 1s and Royal icing—egg white for strength. Do the spoke-and-flower design freehand, then add dots. You will need 22 lace pieces, but make extras. Dry. Pipe twelve royal icing tube 102 roses with five petals for base of cake plus four with seven petals for corners. Also pipe a tube 104 rose for cake top.

2. Bake, fill and ice a two-layer 10″ x 4″ square cake. Pipe bottom and top bulb borders with tube 5. Divide each side into fourths and mark near base. Attach five-petalled roses at marks, seven-petalled roses at corners. Attach large rose to center of cake top. Add tube 66 leaves.

3. Arrange six lace pieces in a scalloped circle on cake top. Attach by piping a tube 1s line on open edges of lace pieces and placing on cake. Frame with tube 1 strings, tube 2 graduated dots and tear drops.

Attach four lace pieces to each side of cake just as you did those on cake top. Above them, pipe tube 1 strings, tube 2 dots and fleurs-de-lis. Serve your breath-taking creation to 20.

Lacy, latticed wild roses

1. First pipe the flower petals and leaves. Pipe individual curved lace petals and leaves as directed on page 38. Tape your patterns to outer surface of the mid-sized flower former. Use egg white royal icing and tube 1s. Outline shapes first, then fill in with lattice and add dots. You will need about 50 petals and 20 leaves but make extras. Dry thoroughly.

2. Bake layers in a 16″ base bevel pan, a 12″ round pan and a 12″ top bevel pan. Fill, ice and place on serving tray. Divide cake into eighths and mark at top of base bevel and just below top bevel slant. Fold an 8″ paper circle into eighths. Cut a curve on open edge to make cake-top pattern. Transfer to cake.

3. Drop tube 1 strings on cake sides and bevel, following marks. Outline cake-top pattern with triple tube 1 strings.

4. Assemble petals for flower on cake top. Pipe a tube 8 mound of icing in center, let set up, then top with another. Gently press points of five petals into mound. Now pipe a tube 5 yellow ball in center of flower and add tube 1s stamens. Attach four leaves with dots of icing piped on leaves. Assemble eight flowers on top bevel the same as center flower. Add pairs of leaves to lower bevel. A fabulous centerpiece that serves 32.

GUM PASTE ROSES

Perhaps the most beautiful of all! Their petals resemble fine porcelain—and last almost as long.

If you've never worked with gum paste, start now, just for fun. You need no special skills—just a love of beauty, your own two hands and the Gum paste flower kit which contains simple tools and Floral-art cutters.

If you've made gum paste flowers before, try this quick, easy and updated method for making gum paste roses. The flowers are breath-taking!

Preparing Wilton gum paste mix

1. Combine one pound of mix and ¼ cup of water in a large bowl. Stir until well mixed. Dust your surface with confectioners' sugar, turn out mixture on surface and knead like bread dough until mix is well worked in. Place in a tightly sealed plastic bag and let rest for 15 minutes at room temperature.

2. Now knead again. Turn out on surface lightly dusted with confectioners' sugar. Knead for five minutes, gradually working in ⅓ cup of confectioners' sugar. Mixture should be smooth and non-sticky. Use at once, or store at room temperature in a tightly sealed plastic bag in a covered container for up to two weeks. If storing longer, refrigerate. Bring to room temperature before using. Yield: enough for 25 or more roses.

Tips on working with gum paste

1. To tint, break off the approximate amount you plan to use, apply a little paste color with a toothpick, and knead with your fingers until the color is evenly spread. Be sparing with the color—you can always add more.

2. Break off just enough gum paste to roll out. Keep the remainder under a glass as you work. Scraps left over after you cut out the flowers can be kneaded back in. There is no waste!

3. To attach a rose petal to its base, brush *lightly* with water and an artist's brush. Just moisten the paste—too much water makes gum paste mushy.

4. Use stiff florists' wire to make the stems for roses. For the wild rose, use fine florists' wire. A block of 2″ thick styrofoam is handy to stick stems of finished flowers into while they dry.

5. Set out everything you need near your work surface before starting work. You'll be able to work quickly and easily, with no time lost looking for a forgotten tool.

6. Green gum paste is needed to finish the roses. Tint a little gum paste green before you start.

7. Read through the directions on the next page. Study the pictures. They are all actual size, and show you just how to form the rose. Have fun!

Flower making is easy—and the results are beautiful.

How to roll out gum paste

1. Prepare a smooth work surface—formica, plastic or glass. Grease it lightly but thoroughly with solid white vegetable shortening.

2. Break off a piece of finished gum paste and knead again with your fingers. Knead in paste food color until the tint is evenly distributed. Form into a ball about 1½″ in diameter. This is enough to make a rose. Place on prepared work surface. Keep remaining gum paste under a glass.

3. Lightly roll out the gum paste ball to about ½″ thickness. Pick up the piece, turn it over and give it a quarter turn on the work surface. Repeat this procedure two or three times as you roll the gum paste thinner and thinner. When you finish, the gum paste should be about 1/16″ thick. The turning will make the rolled-out gum paste an even thickness throughout. Now you are ready to cut out the petals.

Rose beauty *at right*

A simple and simply beautiful cake adorned by a garland of exquisite gum paste roses. Make it for a shower centerpiece, to honor a guest at a very special party, or for an intimate wedding reception.

1. Start by making the gum paste roses and leaves. The next page shows you how. They can be made weeks—even months—ahead of time.

2. Bake the cake—a 12″ single-layer heart tier and a 9″ two-layer heart tier. Ice smoothly with buttercream, then assemble on ruffled cake board.

3. Divide each side of the top tier into sevenths and mark midway on sides. Drop tube 2 strings for guidelines for scallops. Press a 4″ heart cookie cutter into center of tier. Outline with tube 2. Pipe name with tube 2.

4. Now cover both tiers, up to heart and scallops with sotas. Use boiled icing and tube 1s, held straight up. Pipe curves, curls and "c" shapes thickly over the area. Go back and cover top edges again. Pipe tube 2 beading around heart shape and scallops, then pipe tube 4 bulb borders at base of both tier

5. Add the beautiful roses on dots of icing and attach leaves. Remove roses before serving. Your exquisite cake serves 24 at a party or 52 at a wedding reception.

Turn the page to see the rose formed, step-by-step. If you would like to learn to make many more gum paste flowers, the book included in the Gum paste flower kit will show you how.

New way to make a gum paste rose

The fragile delicate beauty of a gum paste rose rivals that of the fresh rose—and the rose is truly easy to fashion in this new, updated method. Just follow the actual-size pictures, step by step, and watch the lovely flower take form.

You will need the Gum paste flower kit, stiff wire, plastic wrap and an artist's brush. For the rose you will be using the three rose petal cutters and the calyx cutter—for the rosebud, the small carnation cutter. Mix and tint your gum paste (page 42) ahead of time and prepare for fun!

Making the rose *shown at right*

1. Ahead of time, form the base for the rose. Break off a bit of gum paste and form into a ball about ½″ diameter. Dip hooked end of wire in water. Shake off excess. Slide the ball up the wire until the hook is buried. Now model the ball into a tear-drop shape. Stick in styrofoam to dry.

2. Cut out the petals. Cut four with the smallest cutter, five with the medium cutter and seven with the largest cutter. Place one of the smallest petals on thin foam, cover others with plastic wrap.

3. Use stick 1 like a rolling pin to thin the petal on one long side only.

4. Moisten the thicker side of the petal with water, using your artist's brush, and wrap it around the base, thinned side up. Furl the thinned edge with your finger.

5. Roll a second small petal on the rounded end, leaving the pointed end unthinned. Brush the pointed end with water, then press it against the lower part of the base. Furl the top on right side.

6. Repeat Step 5 with remaining small petals. Each overlaps half of the petal already attached.

7. Now roll the curved side of a medium petal with stick 1 to thin it. Brush a little water on the pointed end and press to base. Furl the right side of the petal.

8. Repeat Step 7 for four more petals, spacing them evenly on the base and furling the right side of each petal.

9. Make a row of the seven largest petals. Roll the rounded end of the petal to thin, moisten pointed end of petal and press to base.

10. Repeat Step 9 with remaining six largest petals, spacing evenly and always furling the right side. The rose has taken form!

11. Roll out green gum paste as thin as possible. Cut out with calyx cutter, lay on thin foam and roll with stick 1 to thin and elongate the points. Moisten center with water and thread up wire. Press against base of rose.

12. Model a pea-sized ball, moisten top with water and thread up wire.

13. Curl points of calyx with pointed end of stick 1. The rose is complete!

Making the rosebud

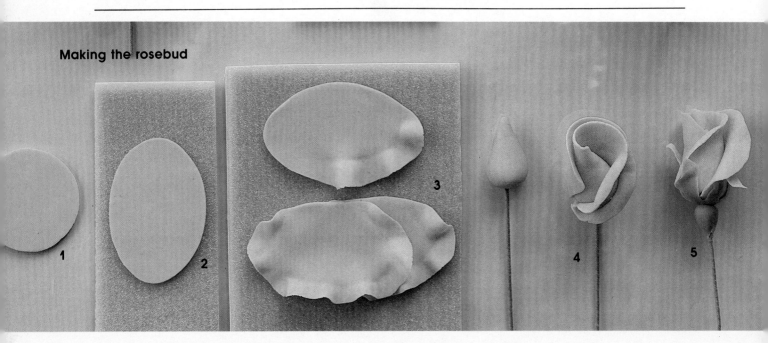

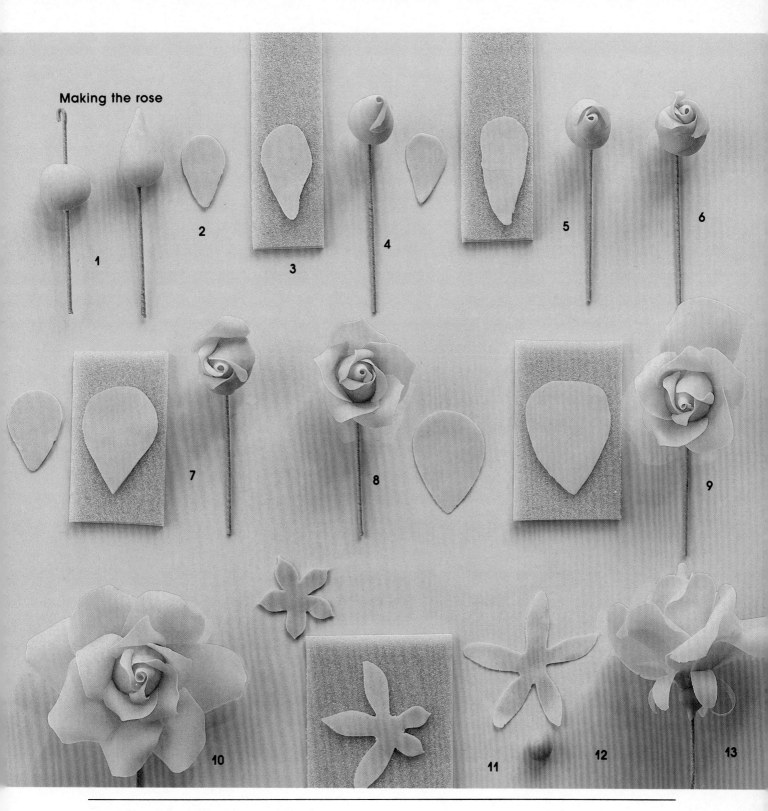

Making the rose

1 2 3 4 5 6

7 8 9

10 11 12 13

Making the rosebud *shown at left*

1. Prepare a base, just as you did for the rose. Cut out two shapes with the small carnation cutter. Place on thin foam.

2. Elongate each into an oval by using stick 1 like a rolling pin.

3. Ruffle the edges of each by rolling with stick 1. Leave one long side unruffled. Moisten half of the center area of one oval with water and lay second oval on it. Press gently to attach.

4. Brush a little water on the lower part of the base and wrap ruffled shapes around it, keeping unruffled side down and pressing to attach.

5. Add ball and calyx, just as you did in Steps 11, 12 and 13 of the rose.

45

A gum paste treasure

Mold this beautiful Easter egg from gum paste—fill it with delicate gum paste roses and forget-me-nots. It's so lovely you'll want to keep it on display all through the year.

You'll need one recipe of gum paste mix. Divide it in half—one half for the flowers and blue trim, the other for the egg itself. You'll also need a set of three plastic Egg molds, round cookie cutters and the Floral-art cutters that come with the Wilton gum paste flower kit.

1. Make the flowers—six roses, plus leaves (page 44), about two dozen forget-me-nots (directions are in the kit).

2. Make base for the egg. Roll out a small portion of yellow gum paste to ⅛" thickness. Cut circles with cookie cutters—3½," 3" and 2½" in diameter. Brush a little water in the centers of the two large circles and stack all three. Set aside to dry overnight.

3. Mold the egg. Roll out yellow gum paste on greased surface to a rough oval shape about 10" x 8," ¹/₁₆" thick. Lay over one half-mold and smooth with your hands. Trim off neatly ⅛" above base. Do the same with the second half-mold. For "windows," press a medium-size egg mold on the large molded eggs to define shape. Trim out windows with a sharp knife. Set aside to dry overnight.

4. Put egg together. Roll a small portion of gum paste into a string between your fingers. Place dried half-egg upside down and moisten open edge with a brush dipped in water. Press string to edge of egg. Moisten string, then gently press second half-egg to it. Smooth seam with your finger. Dry overnight.

Flatten a ½" ball of gum paste, brush with water and lay in center of prepared base. Gently press egg on it and trim off excess gum paste. Form two ¼" balls of gum paste. Moisten with water and press to base, upper part of ball touching egg. Dry overnight.

5. Add blue trims. Form gum paste into a "log" about 6" long. Roll out ¹/₁₆" thick to a rough rectangle about 9" long. With a ruler and a sharp knife cut two ½" strips. Moisten one side of one strip with water and an artist's brush and press to egg to cover seam, starting at base of egg. Cut off excess at top. Do the same to the other side. Trim windows of egg the same way. For each window you will need a strip ½" wide by about 10" long. Moisten one side of a strip. Starting at bottom, press moistened strip to window edge, smoothing with your fingers.

Make loops for bow. Cut strips ¼" wide and varying in length from 1½" to 3." Fold each into a loop, pinch ends together with your fingers and dry *on edge* overnight.

6. Make bow. Flatten a 1" ball of gum paste, brush one side with water and gently press to top of egg. Moisten ends of loops and press into flattened ball. If needed, dampen another ball of gum paste, moisten and press to top of egg. Add a few forget-me-nots to fill in.

7. Finish the ornament. Form a square of gum paste about 2" x 2" x 1" thick. Moisten bottom with water and press to inside of egg. Arrange flowers by forming into two bouquets. Tape stems together, then tape the two bouquets together. Push into the square, clipping stems as needed. Dry. Spray completed ornament with two coats of clear acrylic spray to protect against humidity.

ROMANTIC ROSES

Roses are the flower of romance, so it's no wonder that brides of every age request roses on their wedding cakes. Even the most youthful bride-to-be knows instinctively that the rose is "the queen of flowers" and wants to have her wedding cake graced with this ages-old symbol of love.

Now it's easy to trim a cake with fresh roses and keep them looking just-picked through the longest reception celebration. Flower spikes and florists' oasis will keep roses looking their freshest from moon to midnight—and even later.

There's a bonus for the decorator, too. No time is spent on piping or fashioning the roses—so more attention can be put to trimming the cake with lovely borders.

The loveliest rose

A simple snow white cake adorned with ruffly garlands and delicate lacy fans sets off the most beautiful trim of all—fresh roses. Graceful little cupids, another symbol of love, are placed on the tiers.

Prepare the tiers

1. Bake, fill and ice the three two-layer tiers. Square base tier is 16" x 4," middle tier, also square, is 12" x 4." Top tier is 8" x 3" round. Buttercream is used to cover all tiers.

2. Assemble the tiers with Harvest cherub separator set. On base tier, starting 1½" in from corners of each side, divide into fifths and mark midway on side. Drop string guidelines for garlands. On middle tier, make a mark at each corner and a second mark 2" in from corner. Make these marks 1½" below top edge. Divide top tier into tenths and mark midway on side. Drop string guidelines for garlands.

Decorate the cake

1. On base tier pipe a tube 17 bottom shell border. Following guidelines, do ruffly garlands with tube 17. Drape tube 2 triple strings over garlands. Top garlands at points with tube 17 fleurs-de-lis. Finish with a tube 16 top shell border.

2. Middle tier is done almost completely with tube 16. Pipe shell borders at bottom and top. Pipe curved garlands on top of base tier, marks above serving as guides. From marks on side of tier, drop tube 2 strings connecting with garlands and forming fan shapes. Drop string in center of fan first, then fill in on either side. Pipe tube 16 fleurs-de-lis and rosettes at points of fans. Edge separator plate with tube 13 shells.

3. On top tier, pipe a tube 16 shell border at bottom, reverse shell border at top. Do puffy garlands with tube 17. Drape with tube 2 strings, then add tube 16 rosettes at points.

Finish with fresh roses

1. Set cake on reception table. Attach cherub figure to ornament plate and set on top. Push in four Flower spikes around cherub and fill with water, using an eye dropper.

2. Turn an ornament base upside down, wedge in oasis, moisten with water, then arrange a bouquet of fresh roses and baby's breath. Set within pillars.

3. On bottom tier, push in four Flower spikes between lacy fans. Slant the spikes outward. Fill with water with an eye dropper and arrange roses.

Two lower tiers of this lovely cake will serve 200.

Rose Paradise

Exquisite from every angle! Rose Paradise is the most impressive and beautiful cake any bride could dream of. Lavish arrangements of roses and wild roses are the lovely trim—all are made of gum paste. There's a surprise within the arched pillars—a little cake for the bride to freeze and serve at the first anniversary celebration.

To construct Rose Paradise you will need the Arched pillar set, six 7" Corinthian pillars with 13" hexagon separator plates and six 5" pillars with 10" hexagon plates. Ornaments are Kissing lovebirds, Kneeling cherub, single love bird and Formal figures. The Flower ring is set beneath the base tier.

Fashion the flowers

1. Pages 44 and 45 give directions. Make these well in advance. You will need about 40 pale yellow roses and 150 white apple blossoms. (Directions for apple blossoms are in the Gum paste flower kit.) Spray all these flowers twice with acrylic spray to protect against humidity. They will be part of lasting arrangements. In addition, make 350 apple blossoms without stems to decorate tier sides. Do not spray.

2. Arrange six clusters of sprayed flowers to trim pillars. Surround a rose with about 15 apple blossoms and a few leaves. Twist stems together and tie with ribbon. Clip stems short.

3. Wedge 2" blocks of styrofoam into Flower ring. Push stems of sprayed flowers into styrofoam. Arrange clusters of flowers to trim bird ornaments. Pipe royal icing into basin of Kneeling cherub ornament and fill with sprayed apple blossoms. These will be lasting mementos of the wedding.

Prepare the tiers

All are two-layer. Base tier is 16" x 4" round, middle tier is a 12" x 4" hexagon, top tier a 9" x 3" hexagon. You will also need a two-layer 6" round cake for the first anniversary. Bake, fill and ice all tiers. Assemble with pillars and plates. Divide each side of middle tier into thirds and mark midway on sides.

Decorate the cake

All trim is simple to set off the lovely gum paste flowers.

1. On base tier, pipe bottom shell border with tube 18. Do reverse shell top border with same tube and edge separator plate with tube 16 scallops. Use pillars above as guides to side decoration. Pipe two curved "C" shells below each pillar, then join with another curved shell.

2. On middle tier, use tube 17 to pipe a bottom shell border and a top reverse shell border. Drop tube 16 strings from mark to mark.

3. On top tier, pipe a tube 16 bottom shell border and top reverse shell border. Pipe two tube 18 curved shells, blending together at base, on each side. Edge the little 6" cake with tube 16 reverse shells.

Finish with flower trim

1. Use the apple blossoms without stems for trimming tier sides. Attach groups of flowers and leaves on all tiers with dots of royal icing.

2. Assemble the cake on the reception table. Set 6" cake within arched pillars, then add flower ring arrangement and figures. Use florists' wire to attach clusters to tops of pillars. Place ornaments within upper pillars and on top of cake. Add the prepared flower clusters.

The three tiers of Rose Paradise will serve 190 guests. Present the flower ring arrangement to the bride's mother, the flower clusters to members of the wedding party.

Secret of the Rose

Would you believe that this imposing confection is one of the easiest wedding cakes to decorate? Only basic decorating techniques are used—all done with speedy star tubes in buttercream. The secret lies in the skillful use of accessories.

A glowing fountain splashes within tall Arched pillars. It's surrounded by a garden of flowers arranged around a Filigree frame. Smaller Arched pillars lift the tiers. Two satellite cakes make a unified picture with the main cake by being joined with lacy Filigree stairways. Flowers are used lavishly—but the roses, daisies and wild roses are not piped—they're silk!

Prepare the trims

For main cake, arrange silk flowers in six clusters to trim Filigree frame. For ornament below top tier, fill a petite ornament base (turned upside down) with a half-ball of styrofoam. Push in flower stems. For cake-top, wire flowers and ribbon bows to Filigree bridge.

For two-tier satellite, wire four 2¾″ Filigree bells together. Fill with flowers, "gluing" in place with royal icing. Add bows.

For one-tier satellite, do the same, but use 3″ bells.

Prepare the tiers

Bake, fill and ice two-layer tiers. Make sure that the height of the tiers is accurate so stairways will fit properly.

For main cake, base tier is 16″ x 4″ high, middle tier is 12″ x 4,″ top tier is 8″ x 3.″

For two-tier satellite, base tier is 12″ x 4,″ top tier 8″ x 3.″ One-tier satellite is 12″ x 3.″

Decorate main cake

1. Divide main tier into twelfths and mark midway on side. Drop strings for garlands. Pipe a tube 18 star border at base. Pipe tube 20 zigzag garlands, starting each with a sharply curved shell. Finish with a tube 18 reverse shell border.

2. Divide 12″ middle tier into twelfths and mark midway on side as guide for colonial scroll. Use tube 17 for all trim. Pipe a rosette border at base. Pipe scroll in middle of tier, then go back and add curved shells, blending into scroll. Pipe a top shell border and add shells around separator plate.

3. Divide top tier into eighths and mark midway on side. Drop strings to define garlands. Pipe bottom and top shell borders with tube 16. Do zigzag garlands with tube 18, then top each with a tube 16 fleur-de-lis.

Please turn the page

Draped with curving garlands of flowers, Rose Garland is a sweetly pretty cake that expresses youth's idealism and dreams.

It's an easy cake to make, too—the flowers are speedy five-petaled drop flowers that resemble tiny wild roses. You can pipe them even months ahead of time. Easy-to-serve square tiers are softened by curves and fluffy piping.

Make trims in advance

1. Pipe the drop flowers in royal icing. You'll need about 600. To give a special sparkle, use three tints of icing. Pipe a group in pale pink, then add food color for a darker pink to pipe another group. Finally, add more color for a group in deepest pink. Use tubes 135, 190, 191, 224 and 225 for a variety of sizes. Pipe tube 1 yellow centers or stamens. Dry.

2. Mount about two dozen of the larger flowers on wires for nosegay. Pipe about a dozen tube 66 leaves on wire. Dry, then twist stems together. Gather a yard of lace and fasten around nosegay. Add a ribbon bow.

3. Attach plastic wedding rings to an ornament plate with royal icing. Add ribbon bow and cover plate with flowers, securing with icing. Attach Bridal couple to ornament plate and add flowers.

Prepare two-layer tiers

1. Bake, fill and ice the tiers. Base tier is 16″ square by 4″ high. Middle tier is 12″ square by 4″ high. Top tier consists of an 8″ round layer topped by a layer baked in an 8″ top bevel pan.

2. Divide and mark tiers. On base tier, starting 3″ in from each corner, divide into thirds and mark at top edge. Drop string guidelines for triple garlands. Mark curves for large garlands at corners. On middle tier, mark curves for piped garlands starting at each corner. Divide top tier into eighths and mark 1″ above surface. Assemble tiers, using 7″ Corinthian pillars and 13″ plates below middle tier—5″ pillars and 8″ plates below top tier.

Decorate the cake

1. On base tier, pipe a tube 22 bottom shell border. Frame shells with tube 16. Pipe large garlands at corners with tube 22, smaller triple garlands with tube 18. Pipe top shell border with tube 18. Use the same tube to frame the separator plate. Cover large garlands with flowers.

2. On middle tier pipe a tube 18 bottom shell border. Use same tube for garlands. Add deeply curved shells. Pipe top shell border with tube 16. Fill in corners and between garlands with flowers, attaching with dots of icing.

3. Top tier has "hanging" garlands, so decorate it on bottom and top separator plates with pillars attached. Carry it this way to the reception room, then assemble with lower tiers and frame lower separator plate with tube 16. Drop tube 18 strings from mark to mark, allowing them to hang below base of tier. Fill in with tube 18 garlands. Cover garlands with flowers and add ruffled tube 66 leaves at points. Pipe tube 16 garlands at top of tier and finish with a tube 16 top shell border. Place nosegay, ring ornament and couple on cake and trim lower pillars with flowers. Two lower tiers of Rose Garland serve 200 guests.

Secret of the rose *continued*

4. Assemble cake, placing fountain within Arched pillars and surrounding it with the Filigree frame. Use 6½″ Arched pillars and 9″ separator plates below top tier.

Decorate satellite cakes

1. Place one-tier satellite cake on a 13″ plate. Below it, use 6½″ Arched pillars and a second 13″ plate. Decorate tier exactly the same as the 12″ tier on main cake (paragraph 2).

2. For two-tier satellite, place base 12″ tier on a 13″ separator plate, pillar projections pointing upward. Decorate the same as the 12″ tier on main cake (paragraph 2). Use 6½″ Arched pillars and 9″ plates below upper 8″ tier. Decorate upper tier the same as you did the top tier on main cake (paragraph 3).

Assemble cakes, add trims

Do this on the reception table. Center main cake on table. Arrange flower clusters around Filigree fountain frame. Place bouquet within upper pillars. Place bridge on top of cake and add bridal couple figures.

Have a helper assist you in positioning satellite cakes and stairways. Place one-tier satellite to one side of main cake. Hold stairway above it, moving satellite cake as necessary so top step of stairway will meet the top of the base tier of main cake. Gently push top of stairway into tier.

Do the same with the two-tier satellite on the other side of the main cake, so top of second stairway will meet top of middle tier of main cake. Now add the bridesmaid figures and a few flowers to conceal stairway joins. Place prepared ornaments within pillars on satellite cakes.

Main cake, not counting top tier, will serve 186 guests. Two-tier satellite will serve 98, one-tier satellite 68—a total of 352 servings.

Rose Garden

For a lavish large reception, Rose Garden is the perfect choice. It's a big cake but very graceful, with an unusual construction and roses blooming on every tier.

You will need eight Crystal-clear 7½″ twist legs plus a 6″ and a 12″ plate to set beneath two upper tiers. Four 9″ twist legs and a 16″ plate are above base tier. Four Frolicking cherubs and plastic Wedding rings adorn the base tier.

Pipe the flowers in advance

1. Use royal icing and two tints of pink for all roses—deeper for center petals, pale pink for outer petals. For varied sizes, pipe eight roses with tube 125, 20 with tube 124, three dozen with tube 104 and 14 with tube 101. After drying, select roses for large lower garlands on base tier and pipe tube 9 spikes on the backs. Dry again. Select ten tube 104 roses and ten tube 101 roses and mount on florists' wire stems for top bouquet. Pipe a dozen tube 66 leaves on wires to fill in the bouquet.

2. Pipe about 175 wild roses in varied tints of pink royal icing. Use tubes 104, 102 and 101. Place in flower formers to dry and add tube 1 stamens. Pipe three dozen tiny drop flowers with tube 13 to trim cherubs. Add tube 1 centers. Dry, then attach to cherubs with icing.

Prepare the two-layer tiers

1. Base tier consists of four two-layer 10″ square cakes. Assemble on a double 20″ square cake base, then ice. Above it is a 14″ x 4″ round tier, then a 10″ x 4″ round tier. Top tier is 6″ x 3″ round.

2. On base tier, make a mark on top edge 5½″ in from each corner. Connect with curves on sides and top of tier for garlands. Gently press a 14″ cake pan into top of tier to define circle. Divide 14″ tier into twelfths and mark 1½″ above base. Press a 10″ cake pan into top of tier. Divide 10″ tier into 16ths and mark 1½″ above base. Press a 6″ cake pan into top of tier. Divide 6″ tier into eighths, mark midway on side. Drop strings to define garlands on 10″ and 6″ tiers. Set base tier on strong 24″ cake board, upper tiers on separator plates.

Decorate the cake

1. On base tier, pipe a tube 199 shell border at bottom. Trim each shell with a tube 14 zigzag frame. Using marked circle on top of tier as guide, pipe tube 16 garlands all around, creating a scallop effect. Do top reverse shell border with tube 18. With tube 508, pipe heavy garlands on corners of tier, following marked curves. Do the same on tier top.

2. On 14″ tier, pipe tube 18 bottom and top shell borders. Add tube 22 zigzag garlands, tube 2 strings. Pipe a tube 16 rosette at points of garland. Pipe circle on tier top with tube 16 scalloped garlands.

3. On 10″ tier pipe a tube 16 bottom shell border. Pipe "C" shells with tube 18. Do scalloped circle on tier top with tube 16 and finish with a tube 16 reverse shell top border. Pipe a mound of icing in center of tier and arrange a rose cluster.

4. Assemble 6″ tier with 10″ tier, using 7½″ twist legs. Pipe a tube 16 bottom shell border, tube 14 top shell border. Drop tube 16 strings from mark to mark, bottom of strings extending ½″ below base of cake. Cover with tube 18 zigzag garlands.

Trim tiers with flowers

1. Glue wedding rings to ornament plate. Set in center of base tier and surround with flowers, attaching with dots of icing. Add a ribbon bow. Form garland of spiked roses on tier sides, pushing in each on a mound of icing. Fill in with wild roses and drop flowers. Attach flowers to garland on tier top with icing.

2. Arrange flowers on three upper tiers attaching with dots of icing. Trim all flowers with tube 66 leaves. Fill an upside down Petite ornament base with a half-ball of styrofoam. Push in stemmed roses and leaves.

3. Assemble the tiers on the reception table. Now pipe triple dropped strings below garlands on top tier with tube 2. Top with tube 16 fleurs-de-lis. Set cupids and top bouquet on cake. Just magnificent! Serve three lower tiers of Rose Garden to 330.

58

Rose Serenade

Sweet as a song and lavished with roses and sweet peas! This slender tower of a cake gains distinction from the romantic angel separator set below the top tier.

To construct the cake you will need six 7″ Corinthian pillars and two 13″ hexagon separator plates, the Angelic serenade separator, a heart bowl vase and six little Cherub musicians.

Make flowers in advance

1. Use royal icing. Make two sizes of classic roses—about 45 with tube 104 and 20 with tube 102. Pipe the sweet peas in two sizes, too. You'll need about 350 done with tube 104, 150 with tube 102.

2. Dry all flowers. Prepare top bouquet. Secure a ball of styrofoam in a heart bowl vase with royal icing. Cover with roses, attaching each on a mound of icing. Add a few tube 66 leaves and a ribbon bow.

Prepare the tiers

Each is two layers. Base tier is a 15″ x 4″ hexagon. Above it a 12″ x 4″ hexagon, then a 9″ x 3″ hexagon. Top tier is a 6″ x3″ round. Bake, fill and ice all tiers, then assemble on a 19″ cake board cut to hexagon shape. Use the 15″ hexagon plates and 7″ pillars above base tier, the Angelic separator set above 9″ tier.

Make a mark midway on each side of base tier. Below it, on cake board, mark a curve. On corners of 12″ and 9″ tiers, make marks 1½″ below top edges. Mark curves on top of 12″ tier to define lower edges of "fans."

Decorate the cake

1. On base tier, pipe tube 16 bottom and top shell borders. Following curves marked on cake board, pipe tube 18 zigzag garlands. From mark on tier side, drop tube 13 strings in a fan shape, extending to garlands. Over-pipe garlands with tube 18 zigzags. Add tube 13 rosettes at top of fans. Fill in spaces from fans to corners of tier with tube 16 curved shells. Edge separator plate with tube 13.

2. On 12″ tier, pipe tube 16 bottom and top shell borders. Drop tube 16 string from marks at corners of tier to define flower garlands. Top with tube 18 fleurs-de-lis.

3. On 9″ tier, pipe tube 16 bottom and top shell borders. Following curves marked on top of 12″ tier, pipe a tube 18 zigzag garland around each corner. Drop tube 13 strings to garlands for fans and top with rosettes. Over-pipe garlands with tube 18 zigzags. Pipe tube 16 curved shells between each fan.

4. On top tier, pipe tube 16 bottom and top shell borders. Now for the final trim!

Trim the cake with flowers

On top tier, form a garland around the base with roses and sweet peas. Attach flowers with dots of icing and add tube 66 leaves.

On 9″ tier, mound icing on cake top, extending down each side. Form cascades of roses and sweet peas. Add a few sweet peas and leaves to base of separator set.

On 12″ tier, attach roses and sweet peas in curves to form garlands.

On base tier, attach cherubs to separator plate with icing. Ring bases with sweet peas. Form six cascades of flowers at each corner of tier and trim with leaves. Set bouquet on top tier. Rose Serenade is beautiful! Serve the three lower tiers to 138.

TESTED RECIPES

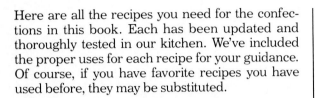

Here are all the recipes you need for the confections in this book. Each has been updated and thoroughly tested in our kitchen. We've included the proper uses for each recipe for your guidance. Of course, if you have favorite recipes you have used before, they may be substituted.

Wilton snow-white buttercream

This is the most popular and versatile icing. It's very easy to use for covering the cake, and stays soft and toothsome. Borders are quickly piped with this buttercream and hold their shape well. Use it also for cake-top flowers. After piping, air-dry or freeze them, then put them on the cake. For most flowers, stiffen with additional confectioners' sugar. You can use this buttercream for writing messages, too. Thin it with a little light corn syrup.

Because it is snow-white, it's ideal for wedding cakes. Add liquid food coloring for clear, pretty tints. Use a heavy-duty, stationary mixer.

> ⅔ cup water
> 4 tablespoons meringue powder
> 1¼ cups solid white shortening
> 11½ cups confectioners' sugar, sifted
> ¾ teaspoon salt
> ¼ teaspoon butter flavoring
> ½ teaspoon almond flavoring
> ½ teaspoon clear vanilla flavoring

1. Combine water and meringue powder in large mixer bowl and whip at high speeds until peaks form. Add four cups sugar, one cup at a time, beating after each addition at low speed.

2. Alternately add shortening and remainder of sugar. Add salt and flavorings and beat at low speed until smooth. May be stored, well covered, in refrigerator for several weeks. Bring to room temperature to rebeat. Yield: eight cups. Recipe may be cut in half or doubled.

Chocolate buttercream

Blend in a mixture of 1 cup of cocoa and four tablespoons of water to the recipe above after step 1.

Wilton quick poured fondant

This icing gives a beautiful shiny surface to a cake that sets off delicate trim. The classic icing for petits fours. Cannot be used for piping.

> 4½ ounces water
> 2 tablespoons white corn syrup
> 6 cups confectioners' sugar, sifted
> 1 teaspoon almond flavoring

Mix water, sugar and corn syrup in a saucepan. Stir over low heat to 92°F, just lukewarm. Do not overheat. Stir in almond flavoring. Yield: enough to cover a 10″ round cake. Recipe may be doubled or tripled.

To cover a cake with fondant, first ice smoothly with buttercream and let icing crust about an hour. Place cake on cooling rack with a cookie sheet beneath it. Pour fondant over iced cake, flowing from center and moving out in a circular motion. Touch up sides with a spatula. Excess fondant can be stored, tightly covered, in refrigerator for weeks. Reheat to use again.

Chocolate poured fondant

Follow the recipe above, but increase water to 5½ ounces. After heating, stir in 3 ounces of unsweetened melted chocolate. Delicious!

Wilton royal icing—meringue

This is the very best icing to use for piping flowers. It has several advantages. Flowers will hold their shapes well and have crisp petals and well-defined details. After air-drying, they are strong and may be easily picked up to arrange on a cake. Best of all, you may make the flowers weeks or months ahead of time—and store in a cool dark place. Then it's easy to arrange them on a cake. Dries too hard for covering the cake. Make sure bowls and utensils are grease-free. Any grease will break down this icing.

> 3 level tablespoons meringue powder
> 3½ ounces warm water
> 1 pound confectioners' sugar, sifted
> ½ teaspoon cream of tartar

Combine ingredients, mixing slowly, then beat at high speed for seven to ten minutes. Keep covered with a damp cloth, icing dries quickly. Store, tightly covered, in refrigerator for weeks. Bring to room temperature and rebeat to use. Yield: 3½ cups.

Wilton royal icing—egg white

This is an even stronger icing than the one above. Use it for piping lace pieces or for Australian curtaining. Use at once, for rebeating will not restore texture. Keep utensils grease-free.

> 3 egg whites, room temperature
> 1 pound confectioners' sugar, sifted
> ½ teaspoon cream of tartar

Combine ingredients, beat at high speed seven to ten minutes. Dries quickly—keep covered with a damp cloth while using. Yield: 3 cups.

Wilton boiled icing—meringue

Many experienced decorators ice the cake in buttercream, then use this icing for borders and trim.

It's not as rich or sweet as buttercream so it satisfies modern tastes for lighter food. Pipes very easily.

Be sure to have all utensils *grease-free* when making this recipe. Even a speck of grease will break it down. Use metal spoons—it is difficult to keep wooden spoons grease-free. Use metal or glass mixing bowls.

Stiffen the icing with additional confectioners' sugar to use for piping roses, sweet peas or wild roses. The flowers are more fragile than those piped with royal icing. This icing is not suitable for covering the cake.

Mixture One:
   2 cups granulated sugar
   ½ cup warm water
   ¼ teaspoon cream of tartar

Mixture Two:
   ½ cup warm water
   4 tablespoons meringue powder
   3½ cups sifted confectioners' sugar

1. Combine ingredients in Mixture One in a 1½ quart heavy saucepan. Place over high heat and stir until all sugar crystals are dissolved. After this, do not stir. Insert candy thermometer and wash down sides of pan with a pastry brush dipped in hot water. At 240°F, remove from heat.

2. Meanwhile, prepare Mixture Two. Whip meringue powder and water about seven minutes or until fluffy. Add confectioners' sugar and whip at low speed about three minutes. Slowly pour hot syrup (Mixture One) into batch and whip at high speed until light and very fluffy. Use immediately or refrigerate in a tightly closed container for weeks. Bring to room temperature and rebeat to use again. Yield: 6 cups.

Wilton boiled icing—egg white

This marshmallow flavored icing is fine for covering the cake. Do not use for borders or flowers. Keep all utensils grease-free.

Mixture One:
   2 cups granulated sugar
   ½ cup water
   ¼ teaspoon cream of tartar

Mixture Two:
   4 egg whites, room temperature
   1½ cups confectioners' sugar, sifted

Combine granulated sugar, water and cream of tartar in a 1½-quart heavy saucepan. Place over high heat and stir until all sugar crystals are dissolved. Wash down sides of pan with a pastry brush dipped in hot water. After this, do not stir. At

240°F, remove from heat.

Meanwhile, whip egg whites seven minutes at high speed. Add hot syrup (Mixture One) slowly, beat three minutes at high speed. Turn to second speed, gradually add confectioners' sugar, beat seven minutes more at high speed. Use at once, rebeating will not restore texture. Yield: 3½ cups.

Cookie cornucopias

A delicate crisp cookie to form into little cornucopias or "horns" and fill with whipped cream or rich Continental butter cream for an exquisite dessert. If you prefer, leave the cookies flat to serve with ice cream or as a snack.

   1 cup butter, room temperature
   2 cups granulated sugar
   3 large eggs, separated, at room temperature
   1 cup sifted all-purpose flour
   2 teaspoons vanilla
   ½ teaspoon almond flavoring
   4 tablespoons cold water

Before you begin. Spray 12″ x 16″ cookie sheets lightly with non-stick pan release. Have at hand paper towels, a large spatula and a plastic tree former to shape cookies. Preheat oven to 350°F. Use an electric mixer.

1. Beat egg yolks until thick and fluffy in a small bowl. In a separate clean bowl, and with clean beaters, beat egg whites until stiff. In a large bowl, cream the butter until fluffy. Add sugar in thirds, beating well after each addition. Blend in egg yolks.

2. Add the flour, in thirds, blending well after each addition. Now fold in the beaten egg whites and the flavorings. Blend in water.

3. Drop batter with a teaspoon on a prepared cookie sheet. Space well—there should be just six cookies on a sheet. Bake in 350°F oven for ten minutes or just until edges begin to curl and are lightly brown.

4. Immediately after removing from oven, loosen the cookies from the sheet with the spatula. Keep warm on the oven top. Roll the cookies, one by one, around a tree former to shape into cornucopias. Lay on sides on paper towels to cool and harden. Work in assembly-line fashion—while one group of cookies is baking, drop more batter on a second sheet and form already baked cookies. Store lightly covered, for up to a week at room temperature. Fill as directed on page 22. Yield: 90 cornucopias.

Continued on next page

Stabilized whipped cream

Fine for filling cakes or cookies, covers the cake well, too. Use large tubes to pipe borders. Add crisped chopped nuts or chopped candied fruit for filling variations.

    1 teaspoon unflavored gelatin
    2 tablespoons cold water
    1 cup whipping cream (at least one day old
        and well chilled)
    2 tablespoons confectioners' sugar
    ½ teaspoon flavoring

1. Add the gelatin to the water in a metal or pyrex cup. Set cup in a small pan of boiling water and heat until gelatin dissolves and looks clear. Stir briefly and cool.

2. Chill bowl and beaters of electric mixer. Beat cream at high speed until it begins to thicken. Continue beating as you add gelatin, then sugar and flavoring. Beat until stiff. Use immediately. Cakes or desserts trimmed with whipped cream should be refrigerated and served within several hours. Yield: 2 cups. Recipe may be doubled.

Continental butter cream

Very rich, very smooth, not too sweet and utterly delicious. Makes a fine cake filling and can be used to cover the cake, too. Pipes simple borders.

    ⅔ cup granulated sugar
    ⅓ cup water
    ⅛ teaspoon cream of tartar
    5 egg yolks
    1 cup soft butter
    ½ teaspoon vanilla

1. Mix sugar, water and cream of tartar in a small heavy saucepan. Stir over low heat until sugar is completely dissolved. Wash down sides of pan with a pastry brush dipped in hot water. Raise heat and boil without stirring until syrup tests 238°F.

2. Meanwhile, beat the egg yolks in a bowl at high speed until they are thick and fluffy. Then pour the hot syrup in a thin stream into the yolks, beating constantly. The mixture will become thick and light as it cools from the beating. Set aside until completely cooled. Beat in softened butter, a little at a time, at high speed. Add vanilla.

Store, well covered in the refrigerator for a week to ten days. Bring to room temperature and rebeat before using. Yield: two cups.

For a chocolate version, beat 3 ounces melted, un-sweetened chocolate and 3 tablespoons of cognac into the finished recipe.

Rolled fondant

This is the rolled icing that gives a perfectly smooth decorating surface. It's really easy to cover a cake with rolled fondant—the material is flexible and smooths easily over the cake in just a few minutes.

    ½ ounce gelatin
    ¼ cup water
    2 tablespoons solid white shortening
    ½ cup glucose
    ¾ ounce glycerine
    2 pounds confectioners' sugar, sieved 3 times
    2 or 3 drops clear flavoring

1. Put gelatin and water in a small pan and heat gently until just dissolved. Add shortening, glucose and glycerine and heat until shortening is just melted. Mix well.

2. Put sieved sugar in a large bowl and make a well in the center. Pour warm liquid mixture into well and mix with your hands to a dough-like consistency. Transfer to a smooth surface covered with non-stick pan release and lightly dusted with cornstarch. Knead until smooth and pliable. Add flavoring while kneading. If too stiff, add a few drops of boiling water.

3. Use immediately or store in an airtight container at room temperature for up to a week. Knead again before rolling out. If storing longer, refrigerate and bring to room temperature before kneading and rolling out. Recipe will cover an 8″ x 3″ square or a 9″ x 3″ round cake. Recipe may be doubled.

To cover a cake in rolled fondant, first ice with buttercream. Roll out fondant to about ¼″ thickness. Dust your rolling pin and surface with cornstarch. Drape fondant over cake and smooth with your hands, starting at top and working down sides. Trim off smoothly at base. Be sure to use a firm pound cake or fruit cake recipe for the cake.

For an Australian method cake, first cover with marzipan. Bake a fruitcake. Set on matching cake circle, fill any cracks or holes with marzipan and brush with apricot glaze. Roll out marzipan to a circle large enough to cover cake. Smooth over entire cake and trim off excess at base. Brush with glaze again, roll out fondant and cover and trim cake just as you did with marzipan.

How many servings will a cake provide?

These charts are guides to the number of servings your festive cake will provide. Remember—a cake for a party or family celebration is cut into ample dessert-size portions. A wedding or groom's cake is cut into smaller servings. Remember, too—the top tier of a wedding cake is usually not served to guests, but frozen for the couple's first anniversary.

Party cakes
These are two-layer servings, dessert-sized.

SHAPE	SIZE	SERVINGS
ROUND	6"	6
	8"	10
	10"	14
	12"	22
	14"	36
SQUARE	6"	8
	8"	12
	10"	20
	12"	36
	14"	42
RECTANGLE	9"x13"	24
	11"x15"	35
	12"x18"	54
HEART	6"	6
	9"	12
	12"	24
	15"	35
HEXAGON	6"	6
	9"	12
	12"	20
	15"	48
PETAL	6"	6
	9"	8
	12"	26
	15"	48
OVAL	7"x9"	12

Wedding, groom's cakes
Two-layer servings are each 1" wide, 2" deep.

SHAPE	SIZE	SERVINGS
ROUND	6"	16
	8"	30
	10"	48
	12"	68
	14"	92
	16"	118
SQUARE	6"	18
	8"	32
	10"	50
	12"	72
	14"	98
	16"	128
HEXAGON	6"	6
	9"	22
	12"	50
	15"	66
PETAL	6"	8
	9"	20
	12"	44
	15"	62
HEART	6"	12
	9"	28
	12"	48
	15"	90
RECTANGLE	9"x13"	54
	11"x15"	77

How to cut a wedding or groom's cake

Always start at the top. Remove the top tier and box for the bride. Remove the next tier down, taking off the pillars and separator plate on top of tier. Slice and serve. Continue working your way down the tiers. Base tier is cut last.

All servings are two-layer, 1" wide, 2" deep

TOP VIEW OF 3-TIERED ROUND CAKE

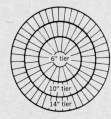

Move in two inches from the outer edge, cut a circle and cut 1" wide slices within it. Move in another two inches, cut another circle, and slice into 1" pieces. Continue until tier is cut.

TOP VIEW OF 3-TIERED SQUARE CAKE

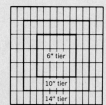

Move in 2" from the outer edge and cut straight across. Slice into 1" pieces. Move in another 2" and slice this section into 1" pieces. Move in another 2" and slice this section into 1" pieces. Continue until entire tier is cut.

CUT HEXAGON TIERS like round tiers.

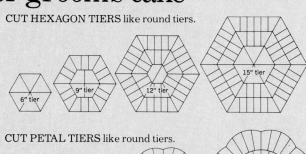

CUT PETAL TIERS like round tiers.

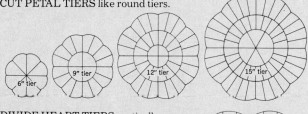

DIVIDE HEART TIERS vertically. Slice 1" pieces within rows.

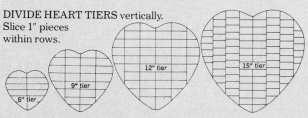

CUT RECTANGULAR TIERS like square tiers.

Round cake

Square cake.
Repeat pattern
four times